D0955404

BALLS
on the
LAWN

BALLS
on the
LAWN
GAMES TO LIVE BY

BY **BROOKS BUTLER HAYS**

ILLUSTRATIONS BY **JEREMY STEIN**

CHRONICLE BOOKS
SAN FRANCISCO

Library of Congress Cataloging-in-Publication Data

Hays, Brooks Butler.
 Balls on the lawn : games to live by / by Brooks Butler Hays ;
Illustrations by Jeremy Stein
   pages cm
 ISBN 978-1-4521-2639-5 (pbk.)
 1. Games. 2. Outdoor games. I. Title.
 GV1203.H3995 2014

 796—dc23

2013032641

Manufactured in China

Designed by L.J. Ortiz

10 9 8 7 6 5 4 3 2

Chronicle Books LLC
680 Second Street
San Francisco, California 94107
www.chroniclebooks.com

CONTENTS

IN DEFENSE OF LAWN SPORTS

A broad margin of leisure is as beautiful in a man's life as in a book. Haste makes waste, no less in life than in housekeeping. Keep the time, observe the hours of the universe, not of the cars.

—HENRY DAVID THOREAU

Like Jeffersonian democracy, religious zealotry, and smallpox, lawn sports were destined for the New World. Stowed aboard the ships of early European settlers, stacked head to toe with the cultural ideals that would come to spawn *Huckleberry Finn* and MTV, lawn sports were fated to find their perfect habitat across the mighty Atlantic. The United States of America was always meant to be one giant grass lawn, waiting to be cleared, manicured, and readied for liquor-soaked leisure games.

If there is one lawn sport that blossomed most naturally in the soils of American life and culture, it is horseshoes.

Never mind that horseshoes were thought to have been first pitched by Roman soldiers and later banned by English lords. There is something deeply, distinctly American about the game. For instance, picture this: over 150 years ago, tattered Civil War infantrymen, weary with war and loose from one too many healthy swigs of recently-bartered corn whiskey, exchange pleasantries around a campfire. Eventually, out of boredom, or out of the anxieties of battle, or maybe both, they decide to pierce the grass of their camp with a couple of rusty iron rods.

They set the stakes some forty feet apart and lazily proceed to toss twisted hunks of metal at them—the steel shoes of army mules, to be precise. The game at this time is still a novelty, yet their enthusiasm grows with each toss. By the campfire, they are hollering and carrying on about "ringers" and "leaners," while their superiors discuss "flanks" and "cavalry positioning" and "high ground" in the officers' tents.

When one of them has amassed the proper number of points to be declared the victor, the game begins again. New players join, while the men on the sidelines tell stories of their wives, lovers, and family and occasionally tend to the fire so there is enough flame to light the playing field. In fleeting moments of silence, as they inhale on their corncob pipes, each man wishes quietly, separately, secretly that the preservation of the Union could be achieved in as pleasant and as bloodless a manner. If only.

Okay, maybe lawn sports are not always this romantic, but sometimes they are.

Yes, there is something uniquely, gloriously American, wonderfully patriotic (in a Whitman meets Southern Agrarian sort of way), about all lawn sports—not just horseshoes, but the entire fruitful family tree. A simple ruggedness in the subtle poetry of miniature sport, in these contests designed for the everyman. This is true even in the fact that most lawn sports are themselves immigrants: bocce was imported from Europe (chiefly Italy), and croquet and lawn bowling were first seeded and germinated among Britain's colonies throughout the world, from Bombay to Johannesburg to Brussels.

Lawn sports and unadulterated individualism share a natural affinity. No referees, no team sponsors, no stadiums, no media coverage, no ten-dollar hot dogs, no labor disputes (well, labor disputes *are* pretty American), no signing bonuses, no team meetings, no drug testing

(certainly no drug testing). Just friends, some moonshine, and the perfect blend of camaraderie, leisure and impassioned competition.

Lawn sports are also inherently egalitarian. They are the epitome of Jefferson's original dream for the New Republic: one vast nation of small farms, a political citizenry of intellectual, self-sufficient homesteads. It is a moving thought. It didn't happen, but the closest approximation of that Ameritopian vision takes Jefferson's agrarianism a step further, carries out the great thinker's dream to its ultimate ends: every man, a plot of land, and a set of horseshoes, maybe even a shed full of lawn games. A country defined not by labor, but by leisure, by subtle flicks of the wrist (and often sizable drinking habits). A nation defined by lawn sports.

Okay, let's break the fourth wall here.

I fucking love lawn sports.

In the eccentric cloud-city of my dreams, in this old, weird America (which is so purely American that it is not America at all), in a small-town just down the road from Big Rock Candy Mountain, lawn sports are in fact the only method of competition—and even the main method of communication. Portly old men with mustaches and overalls intermingle with young intellectuals in skinny jeans and Elvis Costello–esque horn-rimmed glasses. In this gender-neutral, postracial, class-blind world, people of all ages and stripes stand side by side at the horseshoe pit.

Some are working class and gruff, others polished and well-educated; some derelict, others proper in custom and manner (it takes all kinds to populate an imaginary metropolis of lawn sports). But here there is no work to be done. The men and women of this dream-world are committed only to loafing, leisure, and casual competition—to lawn sports, small talk, and cocktails.

This fantasy world may strike some as simply a re-creation of college life, or more pointedly, of my own college life in particular: and maybe that's true. But would that be so wrong? It was a time and place when, for me and my friends, lawn games were held in such guarded

reverence that little else mattered. All of our worries and cares, our regional affiliations, intellectual curiosities, unique insecurities, political pedestals, and class distinctions sloughed off in egalitarian companionship. Granted, in truth we were mostly white, male, and well-off, but with each other, we felt like a diverse and exotic group. Thursday through Sunday, little else moved us to action besides lawn sports. Sex was secondary, to be pursued once there was no more sun with which to light our lawn of sport. Intellectual pursuits were a side matter, to be squeezed in between hangovers on Tuesdays and Wednesdays. And beer was as intrinsic as any other piece of sporting equipment. Yes, our lives were governed by an economy of leisure.

To illustrate this unwavering passion for leisure games, let me tell you briefly about the greatest day of my collegiate life, of my whole life perhaps.

During winter break of my sophomore year of college, my friends and I had retreated north to an old small-town New Hampshire ski lodge owned by my girlfriend's family. Our first day on the slopes gave way to a night of merriment, drunken revelry, and an everlasting game of improvised ring toss, in which various taxidermic wall installations served as ideal scoring targets.

The next day, we awoke to find our snowy wonderland had vanished. The sun had warmed the earth's lower atmosphere to a balmy seventy-five degrees. All evidence of early January was gone. Having originally come to ski (one of the many activities necessary for occupying one's mind when the ground is unsuitable for lawn games), on this glorious day we instead amassed an extensive collection of light beer and played croquet for the entirety of the afternoon. There was no dramatic narrative arc to this life-altering experience, yet it provided a simple clarity unlike any other I had ever experienced. The haphazard transition from to croquet to ring toss seemed to provide a fateful reminder of the truly important things in this world: friends and lovers and cheer, but chiefly, lawn sports.

Since that day, I've been shiftlessly sauntering after that dream: no shoes, no shirt, no commitments other than to your teammates and friends standing across at the opposite stake. Adult life, full of career decisions and social responsibilities, can often make this dream seem elusive. At times, it is so faint that only the smell of rust and bourbon remain. But I press on, knowing that one day, perhaps on this afternoon or the next, this flaneur-fairytale will again come true.

Maybe you bought this book only for the rules. Maybe your only desire is to know how to play bocce, or Pétanque, or cornhole. Maybe you aren't on a quest for lawn-sporting nirvana. That's okay. No need to fret. The rules are all here, along with some interesting history and a few cocktail recipes. So keep your day job and leave the sacrificing to me. The great big family of lawn sports is warm and welcoming. Piety is not necessary: lawn sports aren't selective in who they reveal their magic to. Young or old, big or small, expert or layman, anyone can play, and that is the central joy of these casual backyard competitions.

Don't be surprised, however, if in the pace and democracy of lawn sports you come to find a truer beauty. In our cutthroat, hyper-connected, and hyperactive world, it's imperative that we slow down and reconnect with friends and family. At their best, lawn sports nurture our humanity. They transform a seemingly simple activity—tossing a ball, throwing a disc, drinking a beer—into a magical moment of camaraderie, competition, and joy.

So stop toggling your joystick and get out and find some lawn-sporting equipment, some companions, some beverages, and a lush swath of green space, and let the subtle glories of bocce or croquet or horseshoes wash over you.

CHAPTER 1

HORSESHOES: THE ORIGINAL GANGSTER (THE PATRIARCH)

From outside came the clang of horseshoes on the playing peg and the shouts of men.

—JOHN STEINBECK, *OF MICE AND MEN*

ORIGIN AND HISTORY

Considerable controversy surrounds the origins of horseshoe pitching. Secret UNESCO World Heritage panels, assembled in the black of night, once summoned the descendants of Roman soldiers (who were thought to have first played the game) to testify, but the records of these panels were quickly expunged, the minutes erased, the goings-on too sensitive to be leaked. Promoters of quoits and horseshoes both claim that their games were invented first, and neither side can come to an agreement—apparently compromise being too unsettling for the horseshoe pitching purists to fathom. What came first, quoits or horseshoes?

In fact, quoits and horseshoes are rather similar. Each involves slinging metal objects onto metal stakes protruding from the ground. The big difference? A quoit is an enclosed metal disc; it's thought that it was also a weapon and a descendant of the Roman discus. A horseshoe is, well, the flat U-shaped metal bar fitted to the hooves of well, horses, to protect their feet during hard labor.

The answer to the chicken-and-egg question of which was pitched first may come down to class, or who you believe influenced

whom in the ancient Roman world. It is this vexing perplexity that keeps history professors awake at night. In their anxious academic paranoia, they've divided into factions, with quoits on one side of the library, horseshoes on the other. One tight-collared group believes that Roman officers played quoits first, while the infantry underlings mimicked their superiors by pitching horseshoes (presumably, the infantry used horseshoes because they were unable to get their hands on authentic metal discs). Others viciously defend horseshoes as the original game, believing it all happened the other way around: both soldiers and officers began pitching horseshoes first, and then some civilian copycats came along and formed the shoes into rings. We may never know, but mainly, who the hell cares?

What's important is that the game of horseshoes eventually beat out quoits. By the 1500s English peasants were playing both horseshoes and quoits, and horseshoes accompanied the pilgrims on their trip to America. Pilgrims and Native Americans played it harmoniously on the first Thanksgiving, tossing ringers and leaners along the frost-bitten shores of Plymouth to the scent of roasting turkeys, goose, and pheasants.

In the New World, quoits was forgotten, while horseshoes spread faster than cholera. Well, no, not quite as fast as cholera—that stuff was bubonic—but nonetheless it was quite well-received by the Puritans and their offspring. In fact, several years after the American Revolution, England's first Duke of Wellington noted in his memoirs that the "pitchers of horse hardware" had won the war. The duke surely meant it degradingly, as an expression of ruffled British elitism, but Americans were long undaunted by such snobbery and rightly claimed the game as their own.

It remained a wartime hobby during the Civil War, when Union soldiers routinely passed their off hours by slinging shoes. The industrialized North, with its keenly developed mechanized horseshoe production, had a distinct advantage over the South in leisurely exploits. Nevertheless, despite the game's name, the metal U-shaped objects being tossed about were more likely to be discarded or damaged mule shoes, not those of a proper horse. No matter, play on. Following the Civil War, many veterans enthusiastically brought this most wondrous new game home to their friends and families, skipping their weekend house chores for long afternoons of competition. Wives were united, much like their newly reunited country, in their outrage.

Through the Gilded Age and into the twentieth century, horseshoes remained popular, having spread to backyards all the way from Louisiana to Canada, from New York to California. But the sport enjoyed its most abundant popularity in the Midwest, where the sandy soil was ideal for clunking a perfectly rotated shoe right smack dab upon a virgin stake. Ringer!

In 1910, in the small town of Bronson, Kansas, the first ever World Championship Horseshoe Pitching tournament was held. The winner was the remarkable Frank Jackson. Jackson would go on to become a household name by the 1920s, known for his proclivity to land one ringer perfectly on top of another.

Given this, it's no surprise that Kansas was also host to the first ruling body of horseshoe pitching. Indeed, a meeting in the court-room of the First District Court in Kansas City on May 16, 1914,

gave birth to the beautifully named Grand League of the American Horseshoe Pitchers Association (the GLAHPA). A constitution, by-laws, rules, and elected officers soon followed.

From then to now, the rules of horseshoes have continually evolved and become standardized: the stakes have literally been raised, becoming taller, and the specificities of horseshoe weight, shape, scoring methods, and throwing techniques have been made uniform. Below are the generally accepted rules of modern horseshoes, as we best know them.

And if you're looking to learn how to play quoits, well, keep looking. Horseshoes is the original gangster.

EQUIPMENT, GAME PLAY, RULES, AND STUFF
NECESSARY EQUIPMENT AND IMPORTANT ACCOUTREMENTS

Equipment for horseshoes consists of 2 metal stakes over 14 inches long and 4 U-shaped metal horseshoes no heavier than 40 ounces (and usually made of iron or steel).

To play, you need either 2 or 4 humans or androids, or some combination, plus a handle of bourbon, a case of beer, snuff, cigars, a bluetick coonhound, and preferably a live string band.

FIELD OF PLAY AND SETUP

The field of play can be any open patch of ground approximately 40 feet long and a quarter as wide. Mark off 40 foot-lengths and hammer the stakes at each end so that each stake extends roughly 14 inches above the ground.

For optimal game play, each stake should be placed in the middle of a 4-foot-by-4-foot "pit" of sand, clay, or dirt. in which the stakes are driven into the middle. Sand is the ideal landing surface for a horseshoe. But if you're a casual pitcher, or just lazy, plain old grass will do fine.

GAME PLAY

It is recommended for your mental health that you not play games alone. Divide the 2 or 4 players into 2 teams.

When playing mano-a-mano, opponents stand on the same side at the same stake and pitch to the opposite stake. When playing with 2 players per team, each team divides, so that a player from each team is at each stake.

Flip a horseshoe to determine who goes first. Whoever the open-ended side of the shoe points to gets to choose who goes first.

The first player throws, one at a time, both of his or her horseshoes; then the opponent on the same side throws his or her horseshoes. The object of the game is to chuck each horseshoe so that it lands within 6 inches of or encircles the stake. Once 4 horseshoes have been pitched, tally the score.

Players then repeat this process from the opposite stake (while pitching to the original stake). When playing with 2-player teams, the next teammates on each team pitch the second turn. Two turns or rounds complete an "inning."

Going forward, after each 2-turn inning, the teams rotate who pitches first. Game play continues until one player/team reaches the agreed-upon total number of points and wins.

SCORING

The ultimate throw is the "ringer," which is when a horseshoe encircles the stake. To determine a ringer, lay or imagine a straight edge connecting the tips of a landed horseshoe: if the stake rises through the middle of the shoe without touching the straight edge, then you have a ringer.

A ringer is worth 3 points. However, ringers from opposing teams cancel each other out and result in no points. This type of "cancellation scoring" is found in several lawn games in this book.

Any shoe that lands within 6 inches of the stake (but is not a ringer) is considered "in count" and eligible to score 1 point.

However, only one player/team can score points each round. Therefore, only the team with the closest shoe to the stake is able to tally points. A ringer is always "closest," and if there are no ringers (or there are 2 canceled ringers), then the closest shoe within 6 inches determines the scoring team. These variations can lead to a range of scoring scenarios, outlined next.

A typical game is first to 40 points. But point totals are flexible.

SCORING SCENARIOS AND TERMINOLOGY

Here is how to score horseshoes. Use this exact verbiage in order to sound super cool.

- A shoe that is eligible to score points (either a ringer or a shoe within 6 inches of the stake) is referred to as a "live" shoe.

- A shoe that is not eligible to score points (either a shoe that is too far away or cancelled out by an opponent's shoe that is closer) is called a "dead" shoe.

- No ringers, 1 "live" shoe, call out "one point."

- No ringers, 2 "live" shoes from the same player/team, yell "two points."

- 1 ringer, with either no other live shoes or only a live shoe from the opposing player/team (who is ineligible to tally points), call out boastfully "one ringer, three points."

- 1 ringer, 1 live shoe in count from the same team, shout "one ringer, four points."

- 2 canceled ringers, 1 live shoe (which is technically the third closest shoe) in count, score "two dead, one point."

- 2 canceled ringers, 1 un-canceled ringer, pronounce "two dead, three points."

- 2 ringers from the same player/team, yell out giddily: "two ringers, six points."

RECOMMENDED COCKTAILS

So you're tired of PBR and Kentucky Gentlemen's. What's wrong with you? But seriously, what's wrong with you? It's okay to mix things up a bit, but remember, it's horseshoes, so let's keep things simple. Here are a couple beer cocktails for your playing and drinking pleasure.

THE SHANDY GAFF

This little number goes back to the nineteenth century. It's easy to make, light, a little bit spicy, and refreshing. The perfect combination for a summertime lawn sporting event.

INGREDIENTS

8 oz Pale ale

4 oz Ginger Beer

INSTRUCTIONS

Fill a pint glass a little more than halfway with a good, well-chilled American pale ale (lager works, too). Top off slowly with ginger beer, the spicier the better.

THE GROUNDSKEEPER

In honor of Bill Murray and his character Carl Spackler from Caddyshack, *I present to you this perfect cocktail for an afternoon of horseshoes: the Groundskeeper.*

INGREDIENTS

12 oz Budweiser

1.5 oz whiskey

INSTRUCTIONS

Mix A and B together in a pint glass. It's the simplest of cocktails, a healthy shot of whiskey in a glass full of Budweiser. It's like a Spackler "Cannonball," but less illicit.

CHAPTER 2

CROQUET: THE SOPHISTICATED OLDER BROTHER

Alice thought she had never seen such a curious croquet-ground in her life; it was all ridges and furrows; the balls were live hedgehogs, the mallets live flamingoes, and the soldiers had to double themselves up and to stand on their hands and feet, to make the arches.

—LEWIS CARROLL, *ALICE'S ADVENTURES IN WONDERLAND*

ORIGIN AND HISTORY

In deference to factual accuracy, I must acknowledge that croquet is in fact much younger than most of the other lawn sports featured in this book. Its present-day form dates back roughly 150 years, and its debatable antecedents extend back only to the fourteenth century. How then, as I imagined this great, royal family of lawn games, did I come to designate croquet as the "older brother"? Well, among lawn sports, croquet is sophistication personified, and since younger siblings rarely are, it earns its elder sibling status by virtue of attitude, not age.

The chief adjective here is *sophisticated.* Croquet is literary (from Rudyard Kipling to John Barth to Lewis Carroll), well-traveled (from the Canary Islands to Bangkok), has a seasoned palate (prefers gin, can dissect the flavor profile of a Bordeaux with the best of them), is impeccably groomed, and is always well-dressed. If croquet were to be personified, he'd (sorry ladies, croquet's a dude) look like JFK or F. Scott Fitzgerald would if they were British officers in colonial

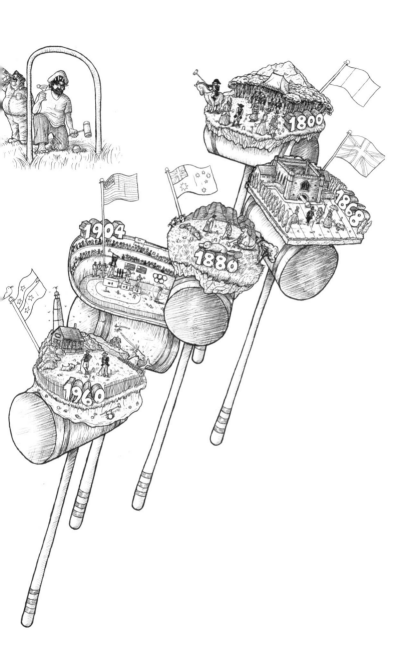

India. Imagine him sporting a seersucker or linen three-piece, accented by a sprightly colored bowtie, and most certainly holding a gin fizz in whichever hand isn't grasping a croquet mallet. Or think of it like this: give horseshoes a good, clean shave, put a suit on him, and you've got croquet.

Even the scruffiest of us enjoy an excuse to tidy up every now and then. Croquet is that excuse.

A relative child compared to its more well-established lawn sport brethren, croquet is no brash, new-money bombardier. On the contrary, croquet possesses the restraint and cosmopolitanism of the period during which it was spawned—that of England's East India Company, tea time, and Henry James (and also, by the way, about the same time a man named Joseph E. Seagram founded a distillery outside of Montreal).

Croquet, as we know it today, first rose to prominence in the British Isles during the latter half of the nineteenth century. Although loosely derived from other similar games such as ground billiards, pall-mall, and closh—all games involving dewy gardenlike playing grounds, wooden balls, rounded wickets, and odd-shaped mallets—the game's rules and equipment slowly codified into something entirely unique and distinguishable from its predecessors.

The All England Croquet Club (later to become the All England Lawn Tennis and Croquet Club, aka Wimbledon) was founded in 1868 at the pinnacle of the croquet craze: the club published official rule books, hosted croquet tournaments, and served as the center of the croquet universe for a brief period during the Victorian era. Providing the equipment was John Jaques II, the descendant of French Huguenots and an early lawn-games profiteer. John Jaques & Sons, modern England's oldest operating sporting equipment manufacturer, still sells finely made balls, mallets, and wickets today. Walter Jones Whitmore, an inventor, wool merchant, lawyer, and hilariously bad poet—like a really poor man's Ben Franklin or something—wrote a series of tactical croquet articles for a heady British periodical called *The Field* in the late 1860s, helping to further legitimize the sport. The "garden parties" of Jane Austen novels quickly became "croquet parties."

Eventually, what became known as tennis surpassed croquet as Great Britain's favorite pastime (two grass tennis courts fit conveniently inside one standard-sized croquet lawn). But for several decades croquet remained a British obsession, and it became ubiquitous throughout its colonial empire, following rich, white men around like a well-trained foxhound—in India, Africa, Australia, and elsewhere.

Much of the sport's popularity is attributed to the fact that women were for the first time able to participate as equals in an outdoor game. Young men, no doubt, were happy for the inclusion of women, and they would regularly knock their female opponent's ball into the bushes (using a move called a "roquet" or a "tight croquet," but more on that later) so that they might use the cloak of shrubbery as an opportunity to demonstrate their hands-on appreciation for the female's presence.

The game also became popular in a former British colony, the US of A. In 1867, a New York newspaper declared: "Never in the history of outdoor sports in this country had any game achieved so sudden a popularity with both sexes, but especially with the ladies, as Croquet has."

In 1882 the National American Croquet Association was formed, consisting of twenty-five New York clubs. In 1900, croquet became an Olympic sport, and four years later, when the games were hosted in St. Louis, an American took the gold. It was never played in the Olympics again.

American croquet rules often differed from English stipulations, as did the equipment. Americans capitalized on the nation's time-honored tradition of shoddy workmanship—it was the Gilded Age, after all—and supplemented Europe's all-wood mallets with foreign materials. US mallets featured rubber, metal, and anything else that could be cheaply and easily fastened to the end of a pole and sold for profit. Soon, as many as half a dozen American companies were manufacturing croquet sets.

By the early twentieth century, Yankees were playing croquet in all corners of the country, on both coasts, down South, and throughout the heartland. But the game was most popular in the blue-blooded Northeast, where Nantucket red and seersucker is like a gentleman's second skin.

In the 1920s, croquet became the favorite pastime of not just railroad titans and white-collared, country-club types but of the New York City intelligentsia, particularly the members of the Algonquin Round Table, including many poets, playwrights, journalists, actors, and actresses, including the first editor of *The New Yorker* and comedian and film star Harpo Marx.

By the middle of the twentieth century, croquet had lost much of its allure. A major recession and two world wars will do that to the hobbies of the über-rich. Then in 1960, that changed. In a much-publicized croquet match, Oedipal-angst was reborn as Westhampton Mallet Club on Long Island squared off against London's Hurlingham Club. The upset victory helped reignite the enthusiasm for the sport in the United States. Nevertheless, some fifty years later, the game remains thoroughly British in character. A small but dedicated portion of Americans have always clutched their croquet mallets with fondness, but this superbly sophisticated sport deserves to have its glory days return again. The summer air is just a bit sweeter for it.

EQUIPMENT, GAME PLAY, RULES, AND STUFF

In our liberal, anything-goes America, croquet takes many, many forms—variations on the basic game abound, though using flamingo mallets and hedgehog balls, à la *Alice in Wonderland*, may prove logistically unfeasible.

The point of croquet is to use your mallet, gold-encrusted or otherwise, to whack your ball through a series of wickets and into the final stake before your opponent does. It is customary, upon victory, to offer subtle and sophisticated back-handed remarks about your opponent's sporting inadequacies. Since croquet is usually played as a team game, with 2 (and sometimes 3) players to a side, you may have to offer some high-brow trash-talking to multiple persons.

NECESSARY EQUIPMENT AND IMPORTANT ACCOUTREMENTS

One of the pains of croquet is that it requires more equipment than your average lawn sport, in addition to a fair-sized lawn. The best way to experience this highfalutin game is to have friends with access to a royal manor complete with groundskeepers who maintain a lawn like a billiards table and a resident butler who doubles as a mixologist—for one thing, such a scenario is advantageous because it lessens the distance you have to travel between your abode and the playing area with equipment in tow.

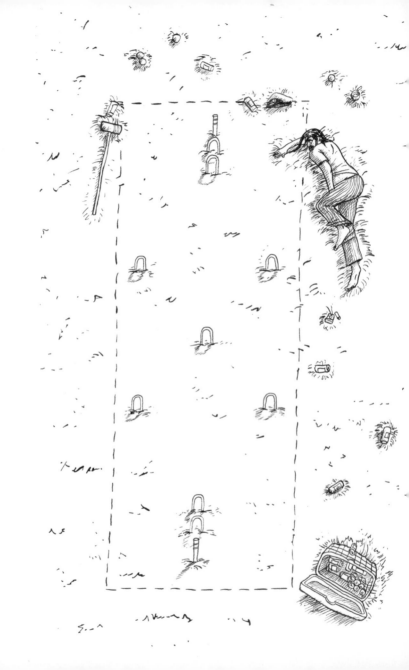

If you don't have any high-class friends, get some. In the meantime, buy a croquet set that comes with a carrying case, preferably with wheels. This saves your shoulder for the game. A proper croquet set consists of 6 wooden mallets, 6 different colored balls, 2 wooden stakes, and 9 metal wickets (which resemble a hardy clothes hanger bent into a U-shape).

FIELD OF PLAY AND SETUP

For the standard 9-wicket game, the official croquet court size is 100 feet long by 50 feet wide. For 6-wicket croquet, which is known as American croquet, the field is 105 feet long by 84 feet wide. But unless you're playing at the All England Club or some manicured South African plantation, just find some relatively flat grass and go to town. Most backyard setups stretch about 50 feet long and 25 feet wide. Work with what you have.

Or, buck tradition and do your own thing. Theoretically, you can set up your court and wickets in any configuration you want. Go nuts. Just remember, in order for the game to function properly, all players must traverse the wickets in the same order. If you rearrange the wickets, make sure everyone agrees to and remembers the correct path.

But if you're like me, and you find it fitting to play the storied game of croquet in the manner in which history intended, then follow the most typical course setup, diagrammed at left.

If you're planning on playing 6-wicket croquet, which is known as American croquet, stop being such a jingoist and pony up the funds for the extra 3 wickets. But seriously, even in America, the most common form of croquet—the variation played in backyards across America—is 9-wicket croquet, or backyard croquet, or just plain, old "croquet."

Assuming typical backyard play (see diagram), setup begins by driving 2 wooden stakes (or "posts") into the ground some 50 feet apart.

Next, set the wickets. Starting at one stake, place the first wicket about 3 feet from the stake, on the side facing the second stake (which is across the field). Place the second wicket about 3 feet from the first, again in the direction of the other stake. Place the third wicket roughly halfway between the 2 stakes in the center of the court. Then, around this center wicket, imagine or measure a 15-by-15-foot square; place a wicket at each corner of this imaginary square. When finished, these 5 central wickets will resemble the dots on the 5-side of a dice. Finally, place the last 2 wickets in front of the other stake, in the same manner as the first stake: the first wicket 3 feet from the stake itself, and the second wicket 3 feet from the first. It sounds complicated, but it's not. Just match the diagram as closely as possible.

GAME PLAY

Croquet can be played by 2 to 6 people, either in teams or as an every-man-for-himself competition. Either way, the goal is the same. Hit your ball through the wickets in the proper order, from the starting post to the second post and then back again. You win by being the first to clank your ball against the starting stake. Similarly, the first team on which all players complete the course wins.

If you're playing in teams, two versus two for example, then rotate turns between teams. So, if Player A and Player C are on a team, and Player B and Player D are on a team, order of play would be: A, B, C, D. Regardless of whether you're paired up into teams, or playing solo, every player plays their own ball, and may only strike their own ball throughout the entirety of the game. Your responsibility to your teammate is to advance your ball as best you can through the course of wickets and back again. Read on for exact instructions.

If you're ever playing with some stuffy-nosed Brit, he or she may insist that order of play must always correspond to the color of the balls: blue, red, black, yellow, green, and orange (if all 6 croquet balls are in use). But really, play in whatever order you wish. That said, it is advised (actually, it's kind of mandatory) that you must keep whatever order of balls you choose consistent for the entirety of the game.

The first player begins by placing their ball between the starting stake or post and the first wicket. The object is to strike one's ball with the mallet and send the ball through the first wicket—ideally, through the first two wickets, since they are lined up. Each time you put the ball through a wicket, you're allowed an extra stroke (or a "continuation" stroke), and you can hit the ball again during the same turn. If you pass through the first two wickets with one mallet swing, then you get two extra strokes, and you can hit the ball twice more on the same turn. But swing and miss, muff, or muck-it-up and your turn is over.

Successfully hitting your ball through a wicket is known as "scoring a wicket." Passing your ball through more than one wicket in a single turn is known as "making a run." As an example of play, say a player makes it through the first two wickets with one stroke and earns two extra "continuation" strokes. Then they hit the ball twice more but fail to make it through the third wicket. At this point, they are out of strokes and their turn ends.

The typical order of wickets is: the first two wickets closest to the starting stake, then the wicket closest to the right, (the bottom right corner of the wicket square you set up). If you don't know what I'm talking about, refer to the diagram. Next, aim for the center wicket, then the other wicket on the right (and closest to the far stake), and then the two wickets in front of the second stake, opposite from where you started. Once a player has passed through all these wickets in order, they must strike the second stake with their ball (for which you receive a single bonus or continuation shot). Then the player must return back across the court, following the same pattern through the wickets, but from the reverse side (since you're now turned around): the first two wickets in front of the stake, the near right wicket, the center wicket, the far right wicket, and then the last two wickets in front of the starting stake. To finish, your ball must strike the starting stake. The first team on which all players complete the course wins.

Up to now, croquet sounds very orderly and civilized. It's not, or it doesn't have to be, and here's why: putting one's ball through a wicket is not the only way to earn extra strokes. A player who strikes his ball into another player's ball (a move known as a "roquet") is awarded two bonus strokes.

Upon roqueting another player's ball, the striker has several options:

Option A: The player may use the two bonus strokes, starting from wherever his or her ball ends up.

Option B: The player may place his or her ball a single mallet head's length away from the roqueted ball (the opponent's ball that was just struck), and then take the two bonus strokes.

Option C: The player may move his or her ball so that it's directly next to the roqueted ball. The player may then hit his or her own ball, thus sending both balls off in different directions (his toward the next wicket and the opponent's somewhere inconvenient). The player would then have one bonus shot remaining.

Option D: The striker may place his or her ball next to the roqueted ball, place a foot on top of his or her own ball, and strike that ball. This will send the roqueted ball careening off into some far corner of the court without moving one's own ball. Again, the striker would then have one bonus stroke remaining.

As if that didn't make things interesting enough, during team play, the first player on a team to complete the course (navigating through and scoring all the wickets) might choose *not* to hit the final stake and "go rogue" instead. A player is not obliged to hit the final stake, and which finishes the game for that player; at that point, their ball is considered "dead," and that player becomes a spectator. However, by not hitting the final stake, they remain in play and are now free to roam the field (when it's their turn, of course, and taking only one stroke each time) trying to sabotage the opposing team(s) and their balls. Jolly good fun!

RECOMMENDED COCKTAILS

If you're trying to re-create what it might be like to enjoy a game of croquet in the heart of Bangalore with your Brahmin allies in the 1870s, stick to gin and tonic. It gives a good buzz and is said to ward off malaria.

If you want to try something a bit more modern, give this concoction a try:

CROQUET GIN COCKTAIL

INGREDIENTS

2 oz Hendrick's gin

1 oz apple or apricot brandy

0.75 oz apple juice

Cucumber slices

INSTRUCTIONS

Shake all ingredients in a tumbler with ice and a few cucumber slices, then strain into a chilled cocktail glass. Garnish with a cucumber slice.

"BALL(S) IN THE FAMILY"

In the following three chapters, you will hear the illustrious origin stories of the family of lawn sports' three most prominent ball games. But in full disclosure, these three sports—bocce, Pétanque, and lawn bowling—share more in common than they are distinct.

If lawn sports were coded genetically, these three lawn games would be close relatives, or subspecies, of a common family. All three involve balls, some rounder than others, being tossed, thrown, or rolled toward a smaller sphere in order to score points.

Their historical evolutions are one in the same. Only recently (in the last few centuries or so) has each one split off from their shared past and developed their own distinctions. In their time together, each of the three sports has enjoyed a variety of monikers. Their rules have been constantly tinkered with over time.

But this is not to say you should stop reading. On the contrary, read on.

These three majestic games are *nearly* identical, not identical. And like the differences between a Peregrine Falcon, a Golden Eagle, and a Red-tailed Hawk, their unique characteristics—however slight—demand to be understood and cherished.

This *is* to say, however, that in the following chapter you will hear the game of bocce described as the brand of ball-rolling with the lengthiest and most glorious historical tradition. This is not entirely true. As explained above, the three games featured in the following chapters all share a common lineage.

I offer up bocce as the prime benefactor of this rich history because bocce is most deserving. It is the most simple and unadorned form of ball-rolling. It is the most versatile—found on strictly dimensioned clay courts as often as it is found on the beach or in the backyard. It is also the most ubiquitous, found in parks, bars, and rooftops at home and abroad.

CHAPTER 3

BOCCE: THE WISE AND WORLDLY UNCLE

Luke, tell Uncle if he gets a translator, be sure it speaks Bocce.

—AUNT BERU, *STAR WARS IV: A NEW HOPE*

ORIGIN AND HISTORY

Culturally speaking, horseshoes is the paterfamilias of lawn sports. It is the most unabashedly American. It's a simple everyman game that crosses lines of class and race and age. And so, in deference to its symbolic significance, the royal we (me and my editors) honored horseshoes with the literary distinction of inhabiting the first chapter and wearing the title "The Original Gangster (The Patriarch)." We stand by these decisions.

However, historically speaking, there is no lawn sport more ancient and storied than the simple act of tossing a series of balls at a fixed target. In truth, bocce is no uncle but the great-granddaddy of all lawn games. From this straightforward but ingenious concept—throwing one object as close as possible to another object with competitive intent—a whole catalogue of lawn games and mini-sports have propagated. We thank you, oh great bocce. You have seeded a swath of athletic competition from which we derive tremendous joy. In this American pantheon of lawn games, you are the uncle only because, let's face it, everyone loves an uncle. The "most interesting man in the world" isn't a great-grandfather; he's most definitely an uncle. And like the most interesting man in the world,

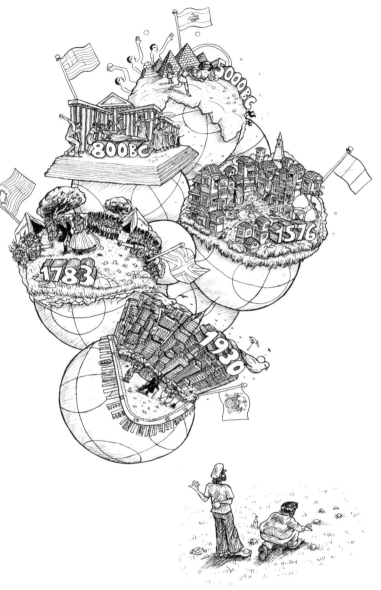

bocce is the all-knowing, mustache-sporting, world-traveling, scotch-sipping, Shakespeare-quoting, tall-tale-telling lawn sport.

Ironically, the alpha-source of modern lawn sports was not developed on grass, but in sand. As early as 5000 BC, Egyptian pharaohs were wandering the desert's dunes playing a bocce-like game with polished stones. We know this thanks to the exquisitely mustached English scientist Sir Francis Petrial, who discovered a depiction of two young boys playing this amusing game on the wall of an Egyptian tomb. The cave mural was dated to roughly 5200 BC. That's one old-ass cave.

The novel concept of competitive ball rolling quickly traveled along the many trade routes between Egypt and the Mediterranean world. By 800 BC, bocce had found its way to Greece and, soon after, to Rome.

The Romans—notorious for throwing stones at people, not at targets—were immediately smitten with the sport. They are credited with giving the quaint ball-tossing game its lasting moniker. "Bocce" is derived from the Italian word *boccia,* which is rooted in the Vulgar Latin word *bottia*, meaning "ball" or "balls." The Romans were also the first to abandon the use of uneven stones, opting instead for coconuts. Eventually, they carved wooden bocce balls from the trunks of olive trees.

Like horseshoes, bocce became a staple of a soldier's downtime during war. The game is known to have entertained Roman soldiers as early as the Carthaginian conflicts (or the Punic Wars). So as the extent of the great Roman Empire expanded, by way of war, conquest, and political persuasion, so did the game of bocce—through Europe, the Middle East, and Asia. Intellectual luminaries such as Galileo and da Vinci were known fans. The game became so popular, in fact, that many European rulers eventually banned the game, believing that it distracted their subjects from more pertinent military duties: archery, swordplay, raping, pillaging.

By the sixteenth century, the problem became so bad that walking down the streets of an Italian city-state entailed a serious risk to one's knees, as bocce balls sprang from all directions. What if Michelangelo's artistic career had been cut short by an errant bocce throw? In 1576, Venetian leaders outright banned the sport, levying fines on those who disobeyed. Repeat offenders were occasionally jailed. I mean, I love bocce, but that's devotion to the game. Of course, whenever there is fun to be outlawed, the Catholic Church is close at hand. Church leaders at the time were quick to demonize bocce, as they did anything that even hinted at gambling.

Despite such laws, bocce remained a mainstay of the high courts of Western Europe. Its popularity spread to Holland, Flanders, and Belgium, but it was especially well-received in Great Britain, where it thrived among the nobility, including Queen Elizabeth the First. Sir Francis Drake was such a rabid fan that upon hearing of the arrival of the Spanish Armada off the motherland's coast and receiving his marching orders to defend his country, Drake, in the middle of a round of bocce, refused. He famously proclaimed: "First we finish the game, and then we'll deal with the Armada!" And he did—badass.

Like every other European thing, bocce traveled to the New World via the wooden ships of explorers and colonists. Given that France was an ally of the American revolutionaries during their war of independence, it's believed that the French version of bocce, known as boules, is the sport that first crossed the Atlantic. However, the British brought their version of the game as well, and eventually the more traditional bocce took root strongest and became most common in America.

Americans, however, chose not to toss their balls on stone dust or sand—as bocce is played in much of Europe—but on close-mowed grass. Some historians believe bocce may have even inspired the modern-day lawn. That seems like a stretch, but it puts in perspective bocce's place among American lawn games: it may have helped invent the lawn itself.

As early as the eighteenth century, a large public bocce lawn called Bowling Green was installed at the southern tip of Manhattan.

President George Washington also built a court outside his Mount Vernon estate in the 1780s.

But a real fascination with bocce did not begin to flourish until Italian immigrants at the turn of the twentieth century began arriving en masse to the United States. Along with other omnipresent Italian imports like eggplant parmesan and Sophia Loren, bocce spread from sea to shining sea. Okay, okay, so it might not be ubiquitous as Olive Garden franchises, but bocce remains a summertime staple for beachgoers, picnickers, and frat boys, and it's now the pastime du jour at hipster bars nationwide. Bocce is as old as they come, yet its popularity continues to grow.

EQUIPMENT, GAME PLAY, RULES, AND STUFF
NECESSARY EQUIPMENT AND IMPORTANT ACCOUTREMENTS

Bocce is played with 9 balls. That's it. The first 8 are the so-called bocce balls. These are usually in two colors—typically, 4 green and 4 red—and they must all be the same size and weight. The standard size is roughly 4 inches in diameter and 2 pounds, but as long as all 8 are the same, you are good to go. The ninth ball is much smaller and called the *pallino;* this is the target ball.

In addition, if you wish, especially if players might become, well, argumentative, a measuring device of some kind is recommended, such as a tape measure or a piece of string.

FIELD OF PLAY AND SETUP
Traditionally, bocce is played on a natural soil and asphalt court 90 feet in length and roughly 10 to 13 feet wide. The area is often buffered by wooden bumpers, which prevent balls from rolling out of the area of play, as well as enabling bank shots.

However, bocce can be played on any type of ground and almost anywhere there is enough open space not to hit other people. Only tradition (not the rules of the game) necessitates a specific type of surface and size area. In America, bocce is often played on any open patch of grass or ground, and even on the beach. Like an official court's wooden bumpers, natural obstacles, like tree roots and fences, can be incorporated into game play.

GAME PLAY

Bocce can be played by 2 to 8 people. Most typically, and enjoyably, bocce is played by 2 teams of 2 players each, but the game can accommodate up to 4 players per team. However you divide the teams, try to make sure each player throws the same number of balls as the other players. If you must play 3 versus 3, it's acceptable for one person on each team to throw twice, to use all four balls.

Whether you're playing on grass, sand, or a traditional bocce court, all eligible players stand together to begin the match. When playing on a court, that means all players will begin on one side, throwing the balls toward the other end. When playing without boundaries, that means determining a starting point, and having all players toss balls from that shared starting line.

Toss a coin to determine which team goes first. The team favored by the coin throws the pallino and proceeds to toss the first bocce ball. In team play, the pallino and first bocce ball must be thrown by the same player, and cannot be divvied among teammates.

Although rules may vary, during court play, the pallino must usually travel past a halfway point marked on the court, but stop prior to a line marked roughly 3 feet from the back of the court, and also come to rest no closer than a foot from each side of the court. If the playing field has no boundaries, or the boundaries are idiosyncratic, establish your own guidelines for where the pallino can rest. If the thrown pallino lands in an unacceptable spot, simply toss it again till its position is acceptable. If the first team isn't able to correctly toss the pallino after two tries, the opposing team has a go. Again, depending on how well-marked a bocce court is, or how big or small it is, local rules may apply.

Once a player, whether solo or as part of a team, throws the pallino and first bocce ball, the other player/team takes its first turn. Their

goal is to toss the bocce ball so it stops closer to the pallino than the first player/team's ball. If their first toss does not land closer, then they continue throwing their bocce balls, one at a time, until one ball does land closer to the pallino than the first team or they run out of balls (whichever happens first). Once the second player/team succeeds in this, the turn moves back to the first player/team, who must then best the second team's closest ball. Game play continues in this way till all balls are thrown.

If a player/team throws all its remaining bocce balls without getting closer to the pallino than the opposing player/team, their turn is finished. At this point, the opposing player/team can throw the rest of its balls, one at a time, and try to get multiple bocce balls closer to the pallino than the opponent's nearest bocce ball.

The throwing of all bocce balls and pallino, and the tallying of points, is considered a "round" or "set" or "leg." Then the pallino is picked up and a new round is begun. Whichever player/team notches the points in the previous round gets to toss the pallino and commence the next round. Play continues like this until one team scores the winning number of points (agreed to beforehand).

Players on a team may decide among themselves in what order they will throw their 4 bocce balls, and this can change for each round. The only rule is that all teammates must throw the same number of balls during each set. So, for example, on a 2-player team, Player A and Player B could alternate with each other, or Player A could throw the first two balls and Player B the last two.

There are no rules governing how a ball is tossed. It can be rolled, arced, bounced, spiked, thrown underhand or overhand, and so on. The only rule determining delivery is that players respect a given starting line that cannot be crossed during the throw. Typically, players will take a large forward step and release the ball much in the way you might roll a bowling ball. But again, there are no specific rules determining rolling or throwing technique. Additionally, balls can be intentionally rammed into other balls (including the pallino);

driving an opponent's bocce ball farther away can sometimes be a better strategy than trying to get closer than it. When playing on a court with set or clear boundaries, balls that bounce over and escape these boundaries are considered out of play.

Finally, for each new round or leg in a game, playing on a court, that new round typically reverses direction; if play begins on the north end and goes south, then the next round starts on the south end and goes north. When playing without boundaries outdoors, play can start from and continue to wherever you want. Bocce is a moveable feast.

SCORING

After both teams deliver all 8 balls, the round is over, and points are tallied. Only the team with the bocce ball closest to the pallino can score points in a given round. For that team, 1 point is notched for each ball that is closer to the pallino than the other team's closest ball.

Only in the rare case where no one ball can be determined to be any closer than the closest ball of the other team will there be a tie and no points tallied.

Games can be played to any agreed upon number, but the standard winning score is 12. Games must always be won by a 2-point margin.

To sound sophisticated and incredibly obnoxious, it is strongly advised to keep score by counting out loud in highly dramatized Italian.

Here is a pronunciation guide to Italian numbers:

1	uno	OO-noh
2	due	DOO-eh
3	tre	TREH
4	quattro	KWAHT-troh
5	cinque	CHEEN-kweh
6	sei	SEH-ee
7	sette	SET-the
8	otto	OHT-toh
9	nove	NOH-veh
10	dieci	dee-EH-chee
11	undici	OON-dee-chee
12	dodici	DOH-dee-chee
13	tredici	TREH-dee-chee
14	quattordici	kwaht-TOR-dee-chee
15	quindici	KWEEN-dee-chee
16	sedici	SEH-dee-chee
17	diciassette	dee-chahs-SET-the
18	diciotto	dee-CHOHT-toh
19	diciannove	dee-chahn-NOH-veh
20	venti	VEN-tee

RECOMMENDED COCKTAILS

Your bocce skills will be exponentially increased if you consume an Italian cocktail while you play. It also doesn't hurt to discuss your favorite Italian scenes from Hemingway's *A Farewell to Arms*.

THE LIMONCELLO DRINK

A great Italian cocktail is one made with limoncello—an Italian liqueur imbibed incessantly by such fictional Italian-American lions as Vito Corleone and Francesco "Frankie Five Angels" Pentangeli. Not to mention it's a really fun word to say with an Italian accent.

INGREDIENTS

1/2 lemon, cut in small pieces
with the rind included

l sprig fresh basil
(plus more for garnish)

Club soda

Ice

2 oz limoncello

1 oz grappa

1-1/2 oz simple syrup (equal amounts of sugar and water heated until sugar dissolves, then cooled)

INSTRUCTIONS

In a pint glass, add a few ice cubes, lemon pieces, basil, grappa, and limoncello and muddle. Add in simple syrup, stir, and strain into a large ice-filled glass. Top with a splash of club soda and garnish with more fresh basil. And oh yea, play some bocce.

CHAPTER 4

LAWN BOWLING: THE WAR-STORY-TELLING GRANDFATHER

Queen: What sport shall we devise here in this garden /
To drive away the heavy thought of care?

First Lady: Madam, we'll play at bowls.

Queen: Twill make me think the world is full of rubs /
And that my fortune runs against the bias.

—SHAKESPEARE, *RICHARD II*

The true lawn sport enthusiast has no choice but to fully embrace the sphere, which comes in many shapes and goes by many names: ball, boule, bowl, pallino, jack, cochon, and more. However, despite their distinctions, the three boules-based sports in this book—bocce, lawn bowling, and Pétanque—are each mere variations on a theme. It's the very simple concept of tossing, rolling, throwing, launching, or what-have-you a larger round object at a smaller round object. Moving on. You may be wondering: when did lawn bowling sprout off of this mangled, twisted family tree? Legend has it that the unique ellipsoidal shape (to use nerd terminology) of the lawn bowling ball was inadvertently invented in 1522 by the Duke of Suffolk.

For several centuries, medieval knights, sorcerers, European royalty, bowlegged commoners, peasants, and others had adored some sort of mongrel-hybridized version of boules. Then one day, so the story goes, the roly-poly Duke of Suffolk accidentally split his third ball in two as a result of a collision with two balls resting near

the jack (the equivalent of bocce's pallino). In one version of the tale, the Duke subsequently used one-half of his now-broken ball for his fourth shot, which rolled in a curving arc around his opponent's balls and cozied up snugly next to the jack.

Another version has the Duke replacing his broken bowl with the knob of a stairway banister and again utilizing the bias of the orb, and the resulting arced path, to avoid his opponent's balls. Word spread of this novel technique, and soon balls were being purposely fashioned with a weighted bias. And therein lies the main distinction separating lawn bowling from its lawn-ball brethren: the ball, in this game called a "bowl," is an oblate spheroid—that is, an elongated orb, much like the Earth, which is wider across one axis than the other. This means that, as these goofily shaped spheroids are rolled toward the target, they will curve toward the heavier side as they slow down, lending an arc to their trajectory.

Then, as has happened throughout history, a peculiar behavior chosen on a whim by some fat nobleman quickly became routine.

Transitioning from fad to tradition over the course of the next few hundred years, the rules and peculiarities of lawn bowling were cemented at a meeting in Glasgow in 1848. Attended by over two hundred players from all of the British Isles, the meeting brought together the greatest minds of bowls at the time. Along with their ridiculous accents, untamable facial hair, and tweed caps, each sportsman brought his own rules, customs, and game-play idiosyncrasies to the roundtable. After several intense days of negotiations, with discussions chaired by legendary bowler W. W. Mitchell, these fine fellows drew up a "uniform code of Laws." An official rulebook and code of ethics was formally published by the Scottish Bowling Association in 1893, with the content mostly based on Mitchell's rules.

Lawn bowling is commonly associated with the British, but it owes its carefully preserved heritage more to the Scottish (the sexiest of the united kingdoms). Over the previous centuries as all forms of bowls were variously banned across Europe, so that commoners (especially

soldiers and mercenaries) would devote more attention to their archery skills. But the Scottish—brazen lads and laddies that they were—rightly ignored the bans. Bowling continued uninterrupted, with lawn bowling quickly becoming more cherished amongst the rolling Scottish highlands than anywhere else in Europe. Such legendary Scots as Sir Walter Scott and Robert Burns were even known to get their roll on.

The game remains immensely popular in Scotland today, though in the United States, lawn bowling is mostly overshadowed by bocce. That said, bowling lawns can be found throughout America. Though it's mostly played by smack-talking, wrinkly-skinned retirees in all-white lawn-wear, it is a game that deserves more attention from the under-thirty crowd.

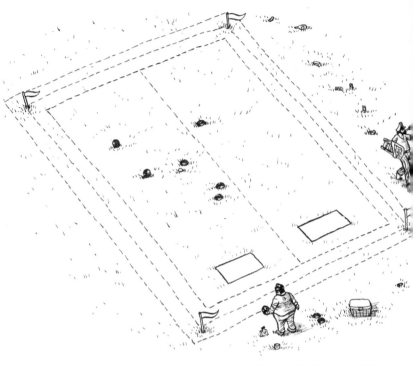

EQUIPMENT, GAME PLAY, RULES, AND STUFF
NECESSARY EQUIPMENT AND IMPORTANT ACCOUTREMENTS

Bowls are typically played by a pair of 1- or 2-person teams, but given some manipulation, the game can accommodate 3- and 4-player teams. Equipment includes 4 bowls per player, 1 target ball (called a "jack"), and a mat that you roll from. In games of singles and pairs, each player rolls 4 balls. When playing 3 versus 3, each player rolls 3 bowls, and in games of 4 versus 4, each play rolls 2 bowls.

All of this is best purchased as a set, since, as you know by now, the bowls in lawn bowling are not balls at all. As in, they are not quite a sphere. Lawn bowling bowls are shaved on one side, which gives them the bias.

If you're looking to save money, skip procurement of a mat. Its sole purpose is to mark the starting position of the game. Other things, like an imaginary line, can serve that purpose if you wish.

FIELD OF PLAY AND SETUP

All the action, if you want to call it that, takes place on a standard bowling green. "What's a standard bowling green?" you may wonder. Well, the playing field is traditionally an absurdly flat grass surface in the shape of a square with sides measuring roughly 100 to 125 feet. This field is divided into 6 playing areas called rinks (they're more like lanes, but it's the British we're dealing with here). Each rink is roughly 20 feet wide and 100 feet long. The edge of the field is often surrounded by a ditch to catch bowls that are rolled too voraciously. Each rink or lane accommodates one game. At a busy field—one within closer proximity to a retirement community, for example—six games may often be happening at once, the whole field busy with bowls. Of course, one doesn't necessarily need an entire field for a single game, so if you're willing to improvise, you can play bowls on any flat and well-mowed patch of grass roughly the same size as a traditional rink.

GAME PLAY

The object and game play of bowls is almost identical to bocce, with a few small exceptions. The goal is to get closest to the jack, and only the player/team closest to the jack can score points during a round.

Per usual, toss a coin to determine who goes first. The first bowler, called "the lead," places the mat—yes, you roll from a mat—and rolls the jack down the "rink" toward the other end of the green. The process of placing the mat and taking the first roll is often referred to as "taking the mat"—genius.

The jack has to roll at least 75 feet, usually marked on the field as the "hog line," but not farther than 100 feet, such that it rolls into the ditch. The jack is rolled repeatedly until it travels the proper distance.

When it comes to rest, the jack is then centered, so it's equidistant from the lengthwise foul lines.

The player who rolls the jack rolls the first bowl. However, unlike bocce (and Pétanque), where the next player/team continues rolling their balls until one lands closer than the opponent, in lawn bowling the players on each team take turns at bowling, one at a time, regardless of the outcomes of their rolls. If a bowl goes into the end ditch or out of bounds, it is considered dead and out of play.

After all the bowls have been delivered, the players walk to the other end, tally up their points, and the direction of play is reversed. Don't forget to bring the mat. Each go round is called "an end."

However, there is one more way a round can end. If the jack is knocked out of play, either past the foul lines or into the end ditch, this makes the game dead, and the round is replayed. If one is in dire straits and simply wants to end an end, you can do this deliberately. It's a nifty move if you're sucking it up and want a clean slate, but it will probably create friction in the camaraderie if you pull this move too often.

That said, if both the jack and bowl go into the ditch, they remain in play. Then it becomes a competition of who can throw the straightest bowl directly into the ditch near where the jack rests.

SCORING

Like all other ball-rolling lawn games, points are tallied for each bowl that is closer to the jack than the opponent's closest bowl.

Traditionally, lawn-bowling games are played to 21 points. If you're playing one on one, that could take as few as 6 ends or as many as 41 ends. You can also simply agree on a set number of ends (usually 18 or 21) and determine the winner based on the total score at the end of the ends.

Or you can play "set play," where winning is based on number of ends won, not total points.

SHOT MAKING

Really, the art of lawn bowling is in the shot making. Like tennis or golf, there are a number of ways to advance the ball down the course or over the net: chips, drives, drop shots, putts, slices, what have you. Much in the same way, a bowler can take a variety of routes toward victory. Here are the 4 basic shots or techniques.

Draw shot: The bowler rolls the bowl out to one side, allowing the bias to curve the bowl into a specific location near the jack, making minimal contact with any of the bowls already in place.

Forehand draw: A right-handed player rolls the bowl out to the right of the jack and curves it back into the left.

Backhand draw: A right-handed player turns the bowl over so the bias is facing right, then rolls the bowl out to the left and curves it back in right.

The drive: Everyone's favorite shot. The bowl is thrown with considerable force with the purpose of wreaking havoc on the jack, a specific bowl, all the bowls, or all of the above. Ideally, the goal is to separate the opponent's bowls from the jack and preferably knock them into the ditch and out of play. This shot must be rolled fast so that the bias does not come into play and the shot remains straight at the target.

RECOMMENDED COCKTAILS

Finally, drinking. If you ever end up playing lawn bowling, it will most likely be with a bunch of retirees. This can be a draining experience if you don't have some alcohol to help pass the time.

THE GODFATHER
Here is the perfect cocktail to pour with liquor pinched from your grandparents' never-used liquor cabinet. Or you can just get the

bartender at your grandparents' all-inclusive retirement-country-club-complex to pour you one. Old people always have scotch and amaretto readily available.

INGREDIENTS

1 oz amaretto

2 oz scotch

INSTRUCTIONS

Pour the scotch and the amaretto into a shaker. Shake it. Put it in a glass, probably with ice. Drink.

CHAPTER 5

PÉTANQUE: THE WHINY DISTANT COUSIN

*First of all, it's not bocce ball, dear. It's called Pétanque.
Pétanque. You understand?*

—BILL COSBY, *THE COSBY SHOW*

ORIGIN AND HISTORY

Pétanque is the late bloomer in the great family tree of ball rolling/
throwing lawn games. However, despite the fact that the modern
game is only a little over a century old, pétanque is regarded as
a respected elder among lawn-sport relatives—deferred to in
arguments and sought for advice in times of confusion.

Pétanque, as one might surmise from its name, is French in origin.
And being French, pétanque and its patrons are well aware of the
game's high esteem, which tends to go to their heads. Even right now,
Frenchmen everywhere are swirling wide-bulbed glasses of raspberry-
noted red wine, remarking of its fruity bouquet, and bragging of
pétanque's unremitting superiority over all other lawn games.

Such claims are, of course, overstated—but not altogether
unfounded. It is a splendid game, even if a bit wimpy in comparison to
its strong-armed brethren.

It must be said, however, that although not a cheap knockoff,
pétanque is a knockoff nonetheless. By most accounts, pétanque
is a derivative of lawn bowling and bocce, and not vice versa, which

makes pétanque a knockoff, a punk, and a rather effete one at that, despite all its bragging.

But seeing as the rest of Europe has routinely marched haphazardly across France through the centuries—running roughshod over its cultural institutions (trashing some, claiming others as their own), and stealing its women, art, culinary traditions, and more—it seems only fair that the French should employ the age old art of forgery and mimic its European neighbors.

The story of its derivation is a sad and pathetic tale—and even the most cynical lawn sport participants should find sympathy in its telling. In reality, this pitiable origin story and the slight equipment and rule variances that resulted are all that separate pétanque from bocce and lawn bowling.

Pétanque evolved from an old French bowling game called *la boule Provençale* (essentially bocce with a French accent). In or around 1907, one of the game's early champions, Jules le Noir, was feeling his age, as we humans eventually do. His joints were creaky, and his back was permanently contorted into strange zigzag and curly-cue shapes. Jules found himself unable to compete at the highest levels—his play had been slowly falling shorter and shorter of his own lofty standards. So, suffering from rheumatism and arthritis but too stubborn to find a new hobby, Jules modified French boules to better suit his now limited physical capacities. No more running and jumping, he declared. Okay, so there's actually no running and jumping in bocce or lawn bowling—no more lunging or stepping. No lower body movement at all, Jules insisted. Players should roll—not toss—the boules while standing still, feet together, in a small starting circle. The field would be shortened by about half, meaning less effort would be required to propel the boules to the "cochon," the smaller target ball that is called the pallino in bocce. His playing companions, being French and more prone to compromise and capitulation than confrontation, gave in, and Jules' new rules caught on and became standardized. And thus, pétanque was born.

Call them pansies for choosing the weaker, feebler variant of boules. Call them saps for succumbing to the whims of a ginger-limbed geezer. Call them whatever you want. They got the last laugh. Over the last century, the new game stuck, surpassing all other versions.

Over the last century, pétanque has caught on with not only the French, but with the many foreigners visiting the City of Light or the sandy beaches of the Côte d'Azur. This lazy version of boules has appealed to wide-bodied, turkey-chomping Americans and the slender-armed, foul-mouthed Europeans everywhere.

The French government even recently declared pétanque to be a "high-level discipline," making it eligible to receive government funds. It's even an official sport of the Thai army. But neither fiscal assistance nor military backing is necessary for the weekend roller—just a six-pack, a set of balls, and some willing companions.

EQUIPMENT, GAME PLAY, RULES, AND STUFF
NECESSARY EQUIPMENT AND IMPORTANT ACCOUTREMENTS

Pétanque boules or balls (if you are tired of saying the word "boule") are usually smaller and made of metal, and each player needs 3 of them. Whereas bocce balls and lawn-bowling bowls are usually differentiated by color, pétanque balls are usually all a shiny silver color and are instead distinguished by markings or lines—one pattern for half the set, another for the other half. Like bocce, pétanque uses 1 smaller target ball, called a "cochon," and it helps greatly in scoring to have a tape measure or piece of string to resolve disputes. Finally, you need a piece of chalk to draw the starting circle.

FIELD OF PLAY AND SETUP

Unlike bocce, which is versatile in its awesomeness, pétanque—being a finicky, picky Parisian by birth—requires a specific surface for play. It is customary to roll games of pétanque on a large dirt or gravel playing field that is 13 feet by 49 feet. In order to contain the oodles of fun you're having, it is recommended that you mark off the playing area with string or chalk or spray paint.

From 2 to 6 players can play pétanque, and teams can be formed in a variety of ways. Because this is a French game, there are really, really effeminate ways to refer to each of the competitive scenarios: 1 player versus 1 player is called "tête-à-tête," 2 players versus. 2 players is referred to as "doublettes," and 3 players versus 3 players is called, not surprisingly, "triplettes." In triplettes, each player is allotted 2 boules, not 3.

Beyond that, the rules and game play of pétanque are almost exactly identical to bocce: The goal of the game is, of course, to score points. Who would have thought it? But how to score points? That is the question.

Like nearly all lawn-based ball-rolling games, one scores points by rolling his balls closer to the cochon. The first player/team to score 13 points wins.

The main difference in pétanque is how you throw: boules must be tossed or rolled without lifting or moving the feet. The usual toss is a reverse underhand, so that the boule has backspin. Pétanque is a game of finesse.

As in bocce, a game begins with a coin flip to determine who goes first. The first player/team chooses a spot on the playing field from

which the boules will be thrown. There the player uses chalk, or some other means, to draw a circle a couple feet in diameter. When the rolling of the boules commences, players must remain within the circle during their turn. Players are not allowed to lift either of their feet completely off the ground during their throwing action.

As in bocce, the first player throws the cochon and the first boule. The cochon should land roughly 20 to 30 feet from the starting circle and at least a yard from the boundaries (if you have drawn boundaries). The cochon is rethrown till it is properly placed in a valid position.

Once the first player throws the first boule, they are referred to as "having the point," or having the boule closest to the cochon. As in bocce, the opposing player/team then takes their turn: standing in the starting circle and throwing boules till they succeed in getting one of their boules closer to the cochon than the opponent. On their turn, each team keeps throwing boules, one at a time, till they "have the point" or have no more boules to throw.

Once one of those two things happens, it is back to the first team. The round proceeds in that fashion until all boules have been rolled.

SCORING

Points are tallied exactly the same way as in bocce. Only the player/team closest to the cochon can score, and they get 1 point for every boule that's closer to it than the opponent's closest boule. A discrepancy over the relative distances among balls can be resolved (when not discernible by sight) using a tape measure or piece of string.

RECOMMENDED COCKTAILS

When playing a game of French origin, go full Francophile—we're talking obnoxious curly mustache, an air of pretension in your words and actions, excessive prissy hand gestures, and of course, a French cocktail. Here's one that's not gross at all.

THE FRENCH 75

INGREDIENTS

Squeeze of lime

1 sugar cube

1 oz gin

Champagne, chilled

1 oz Cointreau

INSTRUCTIONS

Place the sugar cube in the bottom of a champagne glass. Strain in the gin, Cointreau, and lime, and then top with Champagne till the glass is full.

CHAPTER 6

BADMINTON: THE NUTTY, CELIBATE AUNT

Bubbles: Ricky's been losing his mind in here with the no-ciga-rette policy. So I knew I had to introduce him to something new to take his mind off it, so I taught him how to play badminton.

Ricky: Bagminton fucking really sucks, but Bubbles loves it.

—TRAILER PARK BOYS

In comparison to almost all other lawn sports, the game of badminton asks of the competitor a significantly larger amount of physical exertion. You have to move quickly, jump back and forth, leap and stretch. But as several early—and amusingly sexist—explanations of the game point out, "Strength is of little importance, so the game can be enjoyed by both men and women."

Badminton is also distinguished by being the only lawn sport in this book that's also in the Olympic Summer Games—which legitimizes the sport to a level that may rightly make some casual fans uncomfortable.

Still, any sport that includes a piece of equipment known as a "shuttlecock" warrants inclusion in a book of this sort. And so here it is.

During the early days of the game's evolution from rudimentary entertainment to sophisticated competition, the game itself was known as "shuttlecock." Also sometimes "battledore," another great

name. So feel free to ask friends over for a game of "shuttlecock" or "battledore." Especially "shuttlecock." Just say it: Shuttle. Cock.

Anyways.

My hope by including badminton in this book is to return it to the hands of weekend recreationalists. Plastered upon the world Olympic stage, the game has been somewhat bastardized, or at least cheapened. In professional competition, chiseled athletes bring an unwarranted and humorless level of intensity to what is otherwise a perfectly suitable lawn game.

The approach of these nationalistic killjoys is not recommended. Lawn sports should be played for bragging rights, not medals, and they should be played outside with a cooler full of booze strategically positioned on the sidelines, not on squeaky gym floors. It is the game's affinity for the backyard—not Olympic glory—that makes it one of the most popular sports in the world (after soccer and ping pong).

Like nearly all of the more traditional lawn games, badminton's roots can be traced back to ancient Egypt and Greece. Of course, these civilizations lacked manicured lawns, but they had vast expanses of dirt and sand aplenty. A common children's game was to swat featherlight balls back and forth in order to keep them from touching the ground for as long as possible. That's right: the pharaohs played paddle ball.

The game traveled well, making its way along the spice trade routes from North Africa and the Mediterranean to India, and thence spreading into China, Japan, and Siam (modern-day Thailand). In India, enthusiasts ingeniously named it "poona." Say it: Pooh-na! In Japan, the game became known as "hanetsuki." Unfortunately, neither of these terms stuck in Western linguistics. But again, feel free to resurface them.

In the nineteenth century, British officers stationed in India figured out how to turn this rag-tag children's game into a point-scoring contest among men: add a net. And boundaries. And sequester opponents on opposing sides. All decent games have opposite sides, so you can go mano-a-mano, not mano-a-gravity. With this splendid idea—and a twine barrier—badminton was born, then quickly packaged up and shipped back to jolly ol' England.

Back in the motherland, badminton became a favorite among the British elite. In 1873, Henry Charles FitzRoy Somerset, the eighth Duke of Beaufort, held a party at his country palace, known as Badminton, that would have brought F. Scott Fitzgerald to his knees. There the newly augmented shuttlecock, paddle, and net game was featured, and thus earned its name.

Transformed, the sport of badminton quickly spread throughout the British Isles, Europe, Australia, New Zealand, and America. By the turn of the century, tournaments were being held for both men and women. By 1920, there were three hundred official badminton clubs in England. By 1930 there were five hundred. And by the time World War II was over, nine thousand badminton clubs were spread throughout the British Isles.

Since then, the sport has established an international governing body and, as I've said, become all official, with tournaments and world champions and the rest of it. Don't be fooled. Badminton belongs in the backyard, where strength, and skill, are of little importance.

EQUIPMENT, GAME PLAY, RULES, AND STUFF

Badminton is simple: it's like a cross between tennis and volleyball. Only the rackets are twee and you're smacking a weighted feathered thingy that looks like a fairy (it's called a shuttle or shuttlecock, as you know by now). Like volleyball, the object is to hit the shuttle over the net so that it lands in your opponent's court before it can be returned, with no bounces allowed. You can wail on the shuttle however you like: smash it with maximum power (break someone's nose) or use the most delicate touch to win (a more humane manner with which to embarrass an opponent).

NECESSARY EQUIPMENT AND IMPORTANT ACCOUTREMENTS

Badminton requires special rackets, 1 for each player. Then you need a net (and a way to secure the net), and something to mark the court boundaries: string, chalk, a line of beer cans, whatever. And shuttlecocks.

FIELD OF PLAY AND SETUP

Don't worry about creating a perfectly lined and segmented badminton court. If you're looking to get official with your badminton play, I'd prefer and recommend you not use this book as a vehicle. All you need to play is a patch of grass measuring roughly 20 feet by 40 or 50 feet. After putting up the net, which should be about 5 feet high, mark boundaries approximating this area using chalk or paint or string.

Badminton uses 2 or 4 players. Games can be played 1 on 1, but the most enjoyable way is 2 versus 2. Toss a coin to decide which side will serve first and which receive first.

Like tennis, the server stands at the baseline, on the right side, and hits the shuttlecock diagonally over the net to the opponent, who is on their right side. On an official court, each side is divided into two service boxes, and you have to serve into the diagonally opposite service box. Casual backyard games rarely mark service boxes, so just be friendly and serve to where the service box would have been if you cared about such things.

Like amateur gym-class volleyball, you may only serve underhand, though otherwise overhand strikes are okay.

    Like tennis, a player/team can hit the shuttlecock only once to return it over the net. If a player/team hits the shuttlecock into the net or it lands on their own side or anywhere out of bounds, they lose the rally. If someone receiving the shuttlecock lets it hit the ground within bounds on their side of the court, they lose the rally. If someone hits the shuttlecock before it crosses to their side of the net, they lose the rally (aka, no reaching over the net). If someone lets the shuttlecock hit their body, they lose the rally. Hear that? Beam right at your opponent and you can leave a bruise and win the rally. See how much fun this game can be?

Like volleyball, points can only be scored by the team that's serving. Not serving yet? Regain service control by winning the rally when your opponent is serving. (Reference the "Scoring" section for rules on how to win points and rallies.)

Here's a tip: for maximum amusement, don't try to score immediately off the serve. It's more fun to rally, hitting the shuttlecock back and forth over the net. Sure, the ultimate object is still to win. But win with style. Don't just lob up sitting ducks for them to smack back at you. Try placing the shuttle in the deep corners of your opponent's court. Make them scramble.

SCORING

Only the serving player/team can score points, and you score 1 point for winning a rally. Points are scored when you're serving and your opponent hits the shuttlecock out of bounds or into the net, hits it before it is able to cross the net, or allows the shuttlecock to strike his body or hit the ground before he's able to connect his racket to it.

Traditionally, games are played to 15 points. If the score becomes a painstakingly close 14 to 14, the player/team who reaches 14 first gets to decide whether to set the final score at 15 or 17. Matches are usually played as the best 2 out of 3 games.

RECOMMENDED COCKTAILS

If you're going to wear tennis whites and play a hoity-toity game like badminton, then you might as well get drunk off one of the more snobbish drinks east of the Atlantic. Pimm's is a fruity, gingery gin-based liqueur, and a Pimm's Cup is the most traditional way to enjoy this fine elixir. It is traditionally served with lemonade. An excellent variation is the Pimm's Royal Cup, which substitutes Champagne (or sparkling white wine) for the lemonade.

PIMM'S CUP

INGREDIENTS

1 slice lemon

1 slice cucumber

1 slice orange

1 slice apple

1 sprig fresh mint

4 oz. lemonade, lemon-lime soda, or ginger ale

2 oz. Pimm's liqueur No. 1

INSTRUCTIONS

Lightly muddle the fruit slices and mint in the bottom of the glass. Or don't. If you're feeling lazy, just put them in the glass and pour the lemonade and Pimm's over them. Swirl it around. Chug-a-lug.

CHAPTER 7

CORNHOLE: THE HILLBILLY ADOPTED THIRD COUSIN

Peter . . . watch out for your cornhole, bud.

— LAWRENCE, *OFFICE SPACE*

Cornhole is not my favorite lawn game. In my estimation it's ubiquitous and dull. It's the beer hat of lawn games, its uniform consisting of Ed Hardy t-shirts and extra-large NFL jerseys, and it's routinely played on concrete. But it is immensely popular at sporting events and fraternal organizations across the country, and it regularly accompanies an activity I cherish nearly as much as lawn-sporting: tailgating.

I'd considered not including cornhole, but since it shows up at most parties whether you like it or not, I have deferred to the American people. And so, with populist sentiments winning out, I give you cornhole.

The origin of cornhole goes mostly undiscussed by serious East Coast scholars. They have better things to do, like translate ancient hieroglyphics, speak in stuffy affected accents, and play croquet. But in the Midwest, professors are less bothered by pestilent things like high culture, and so apparently feel that tracing the antecedents of a game featuring corn-filled bags tossed into small, round holes is perfectly good fun.

There is damn little evidence that cornhole is anything but a modern fascination. What miniscule historical evidence there is, cornhole enthusiasts have found it, dissected it, sewn it back together, magnified it, twisted it, and turned it into the basis of several competing cornhole creation myths.

The most common theory of cornhole's genesis goes all the way back to the fourteenth century. In this enchanting tale, in 1325, a soft-spoken German cabinetmaker named Matthias Kaupermann was out for a midmorning stroll through the foothills of the Alps when he came upon several children throwing rocks into a hole in the ground. No doubt, his first thoughts concerned the general intelligence of German children: "I mean, really, throwing rocks in a hole?" But then Matthias's more compassionate side spurred him to action: tossing jagged chunks of granite around might not be the safest way for these kids to spend their free time, and so Matthias decided to create a safer version.

Of course, the logical replacement for a rock is a little cloth sack filled with dried corn kernels. Lucky for Matthias, Bavaria was a cornucopia of corn. Matthias returned home and sewed and stuffed several bags and, the very next day, delivered his newly stitched corn-filled satchels to the grateful children. No longer would they have to suffer bloody temples and bruised shins from errant throws. The children were delighted.

Scholars, if that's the right word, propose that Matthias's game caught on in the Rhineland and made its way to America by German immigrants. We're still waiting for the evidence.

If it is true, we have much to thank Matthias Kaupermann for. Imagine if cornhole, or rockhole, had evolved to its present day status with three-pound stones remaining the constant in the game's changing array of equipment. Instead of NASCAR races filled with thousands of drunk idiots, we'd have NASCAR races filled with thousands of drunk idiots armed with stones.

But this logic escaped most of cornhole's historians.

Strangely, despite a shared love of sausage, sauerkraut, and sporting safety, not all Midwest academics accept this account—especially those living outside of Ohio.

They had another theory—their own, homegrown theory.

In this telling, a single Midwestern farmer with a name seemingly destined for sporting greatness or a starring role in the New Testament—Jebediah McGillicuddy—is credited with masterminding the game of cornhole in his barn in the middle of the nineteenth century. Jebediah and his friends would pass the time with these contests in between rolling bales of hay and tending to the cornfields. However, they apparently never discussed their passion outside the walls of McGillicuddy's barn, since there is little evidence that Jebediah McGillicuddy and his American-bred game of cornhole ever really existed.

Was the story of McGillicuddy simply the xenophobic fantasy of certain overly patriotic cornhole scholars unwilling to accept the foreign-born nature of their favorite game? We may never know.

But true lawn game enthusiasts understand the importance of embracing history in all its complex intricacies and troubling shades of gray.

What is undoubtedly true is that cornhole's renaissance in popular sporting culture—its arrival on the Great Lawn of Sports—didn't come until the 1990s, and logically so. What better mini-game accompaniment to a blaring rendition of "Smells Like Teen Spirit," American-made microbrews, cutoff jeans, and spiked hair, than chucking bags of corn into a cut-out hole in a slanted wooden board? That is a rhetorical question, but I'll answer it anyway: nothing. There is no better accompaniment.

Equally undeniable, cornhole's modern rebirth is credited to an enthusiastic bunch in and around Cincinnati. Why? If we were being unkind, we might say it was because there's nothing better to do in and around Cincinnati.

It pains me greatly to offer any sort of kudos to Cincinnati—or any city, town, or place within the confines of Ohio—even for a game as forgettable as cornhole. But I give credit where credit is due (in this case, anyway).

It's not quite clear who or what inspired this rebirth. No one knows why or how it happened. Perhaps it was reimagined by several stoned friends over bowls of that awful spaghetti-chili Cincinnatians are so fond of. Perhaps, interested in their German heritage, third-generation Cincinnatians peered back through the annals of time, found Matthias's priceless invention, and claimed it as their own.

However it got here, we're stuck with it now. It's everywhere, unavoidable. So give cornhole a try. Maybe you won't hate it.

EQUIPMENT, GAME PLAY, RULES, AND STUFF
NECESSARY EQUIPMENT AND IMPORTANT ACCOUTREMENTS

For such a simple concept, cornhole is kind of a pain in the ass. In order to play, you need 2 heavy wooden boards on 4 legs with a slight slant from back to front and a round hole in the middle. Unlike most lawn games, which can be neatly packaged into portable carrying cases, bulky wooden boards take up a fair amount of storage space. Kind of impractical, right?

But, okay, I don't have to explain this to you. If you're savvy and hip enough to have picked up this book (the threshold is low), you know what a cornhole board looks like. And you probably have a pretty good idea of where to procure one. If cornhole means that much to you, go get a set at your local sports equipment store; it's really the only reasonable option.

If you don't feel like buying one, then your only other option is to build a set yourself. There aren't really any everyday household items that could substitute for the real thing. I suppose you could just grab some rocks and dig a couple holes in the ground like those German kids did, but that just seems sad.

If you're feeling handy and want to build your own set, here are some dimensions to keep in mind: a cornhole board should be roughly 2 by 4 feet; the front end should sit approximately 3 inches off the ground, while the back end should rise roughly a foot off the ground. The all-important hole in the middle of the board should be 6 inches in diameter and positioned 9 inches from the back of the board. Hey, maybe it will be fun. You can paint it your alma mater's colors, invite over your old college buddies, and make a day of it. Fun.

Right, of course. You need something to slam into the hole. You need bags of corn, or corn-bags, or corn-sacks. You can substitute rice, or seeds, or beans, but then you aren't playing cornhole. You're playing ricehole. Totally different game. Anyways, these sacks of corn typically measure 6 inches by 6 inches and weigh between 14 and 16 ounces. As before, you need 8 bags in 2 colors of 4 each. Now you're ready.

FIELD OF PLAY AND SETUP

Set your 2 cornhole boards facing each other roughly 25 to 30 feet apart.

GAME PLAY

Cornhole can be played by 2 or 4 people. While 1 on 1 is acceptable, I suppose, in all honesty, cornhole played right is always 2 versus 2.

Players/teams arrange themselves just like in horseshoes, and game play unfolds the same way. In doubles, team members stand opposite each other at each board. An inning begins with an initial pitch of one corn-bag to the opposing platform. The only rule governing the throw is that players must not step past the front of their board during their throwing motion. Otherwise—lob it, beam it, underhand, overhand, side arm, you name it.

The goal, of course, is to slot the bag into the hole in the opposing board. However, bags on top of the board also count for points, so it is perfectly acceptable and applaudable to plop a bag smack dab on top. Opponents on the same side alternate turns throwing bags one at a

time until all 8 bags have been tossed. This is considered the top half of an inning. Following the initial eight pitches, the opponents on the other side pick up the bags and pitch back, completing the bottom half of the inning.

SCORING

A "corn-bag-in-the-hole," sometimes called a "hole-in," is scored as 3 points. It doesn't matter how the bag gets in the hole: it can be tossed through directly, slide in, ricochet off another bag, or be bumped in by another toss.

A corn-bag that comes to rest on the platform is "in-the-count" or "on-the-board" and is worth 1 point. If a corn-bag bounces off the ground and onto the board, it's considered a foul and is removed from the platform.

A corn-bag anywhere else has no value.

Like horseshoes, cornhole uses "cancellation scoring," but it eliminates any "who's closest to the post" measuring controversies. Counting, apparently, is challenge enough in this game. Essentially, after 8 bags are thrown, each team counts up their point-earning bags. Then the lesser total is subtracted from the higher total, and the team with the higher total scores only the points that are left over. That is, only one team earns points in any given half inning, and they only earn those points that exceed the point-earning corn-bags of the opponent.

For instance: if one team puts a bag through the hole, and the other team does as well, and all other bags miss the platform entirely, then no points are scored. Or if one team scores a hole-in (for 3 points), and the other puts 2 on-the-board (for 2 points), then the team with the hole-in scores 1 point.

In other words, here is cornhole's simple point-scoring equation: most points – fewer points = earned points (awarded to the deserving team).

Whichever player/team scored the last point begins the next frame of play.

The game continues until one team amasses 21 points. Some people play that a team must score exactly 21 points. But not everyone does; it's up to you.

RECOMMENDED COCKTAILS

If you're going to play cornhole, you're going to need to get insanely drunk before, during, and afterward. Cornhole has a certain redneck/fraternity vibe, even when no rednecks or frat brothers are actually playing, so it's important for you to fit in by consuming significant amounts of alcohol. What better way to do that than by throwing together a random assortment of liquors and calling it a cocktail? In other words, mix up an extra-strong Long Island Iced Tea.

LONG ISLAND ICED TEA

INGREDIENTS

Sliced lemon   Splash of cola   **2 oz.** triple sec

2 oz. gin

2 oz. tequila

2 oz. rum

3 oz. sweet-and-sour mix

2 oz. vodka

INSTRUCTIONS

Mix ingredients together over ice in a glass. Pour into a shaker, give it a couple strong shakes, and pour back into the glass. Garnish with lemon and chug.

CHAPTER 8

POLISH HORSESHOES: THE DRUNK UNCLE, ONCE REMOVED

Don't you see what Whatley is after? Total joke-telling immunity! He's already got the big two religions covered. If he ever gets Polish citizenship, there'll be no stopping him.

— JERRY SEINFELD, IN "THE YADA YADA" (*SEINFELD*)

Beer bottles, filled with just a bit of sand, are balanced delicately atop yellow Wiffle ball bats. The bats protrude from the loose surfside sand on a glorious summer day at the beach. The bottle glistens in the sun. Children shout in the surf. A flying disc, a Frisbee, sails toward the precariously placed bottle. Doink! A direct hit. High fives ensue, and the bottle is restored for another round.

This is just a momentary slice of the action in the game of Polish horseshoes. One to be savored.

Lawn game classicists may be upset to find Polish horseshoes included in this book. It doesn't entirely fit the bill—having originated on the beach, not a lawn. But this is my book, and I make the rules. And while I feel no obligation to justify its consecration here, I will anyways.

Admittedly, the history of Polish horseshoes is neither lengthy nor distinguished, and no one can quite agree on what to call it. In some places, it's called Spanish horseshoes (and perhaps, reflecting the prevailing xenophobia in your hometown, you've heard it by another name). Midwesterners call it Frisbeener. Virginians refer to it as French Darts. And in Canada, it's known as Beersbee.

Where did it come from? No one can say. The game seems to have emerged simultaneously and spontaneously in various cities, states, and towns across North America. Most likely, it evolved from time-wasting novelties at campgrounds, ultimate Frisbee tournaments, fraternity house front yards, and beach picnics—at any place, that is, where young folks might gather outside while under the influence—until all its elements converged into the current contest. Here's what we know: someone, somewhere, in the not-too-distant past, thought of it, and now it's here to stay.

But not all great things must be old. Sure expansion teams and shoddy suburban McMansions are nauseating, to say the least. But iPhones are pretty great. MTV was good while it lasted. Taste-bud-tingling microbrews are literally bubbling from public fountains. And beer pong. All are comforts of our post-postmodern existence.

Besides, what Polish horseshoes lacks in historical pedigree, it more than makes up for in creative genius. Polish horseshoes is a case study in lawn game hybridity. A game combining Wiffle ball bats, a Frisbee, beer, beer bottles, and sand, Polish horseshoes is like a stoned Frat-boy's wet dream gone to South Beach. That may not sound all that appealing at first, but as they say: once you go Polish . . . you'll be like, "Hey, we should do this Polish thing more often." Okay, no one has ever said that. But really, Polish horseshoes seems to have that kind of coo-coo effect on people.

If Polish horseshoes is more than the sum of its parts, it's worth knowing where two of its parts come from: Wiffle ball bats and Frisbees, which for the first time join in this glorious matrimony of lawn-sportage. Yes, lawn-sportage is a word.

In 1953, the Wiffle ball was invented in the backyard of David N. Mullany in Fairfield, Connecticut. Mullany was trying to help his kid learn to throw a curveball, and he discovered that if you just took a hollow ball and cut a bunch of holes in it, any twelve year old can chuck Sandy Koufax-esque curves, sinkers, and sliders. Not to mention: Light, plastic baseballs can't break Mr. George Everett

Wilson Sr.'s windows or be hit into the yard with the giant frothing-at-the-mouth English mastiff known as "the Beast." Wiffle ball caught on in the Mid-Atlantic region, and soon yellow plastic bats were needed to hit Wiffle balls, and a legend was born.

Meanwhile, farther north, university students were smoking way too much pot and looking for ways to amuse themselves in between art classes. Coincidentally, the Frisbie Baking Company of Bridgeport, Connecticut, was churning out hot cherry, blackberry, and blueberry pies that were sold to many New England colleges and delivered just in time for the afternoon munchies. Hungry, stoned, and surprisingly intuitive, coeds quickly realized that a pie tin emptied of its fruity, crusty goodness could be turned over and tossed for fun. Eventually, some opportunistic jerk in Los Angeles made a plastic version, changed the name slightly to avoid a lawsuit, and took all the credit and the money. Such is capitalism. On the bright side, the Frisbee was born.

And today, to whoever is responsible for bringing Frisbees, Wiffle ball bats, and beer together, we owe everlasting gratitude.

EQUIPMENT, GAME PLAY, RULES, AND STUFF

The object of Polish horseshoes is to knock the bottle off the top of a Wiffle ball bat with a Frisbee, either with a direct hit or by striking the bat upon which the bottle rests.

NECESSARY EQUIPMENT AND ACCOUTREMENTS

With the Internet and what not, you can order a set of plastic thingamajiggers specifically made for Polish horseshoes. But a true lawn sport enthusiast should have all the materials already on hand.

- Everyone should have a Frisbee

- Everyone should have several Wiffle ball bats—you need at least two for Polish horseshoes. If you don't have Wiffle ball bats, a pair of ski poles can also work, or a couple of wooden stakes, tiki torches, or 2 of any polelike object that can be stuck in the ground and upon which a beer bottle may be balanced.

- 2 empty beer bottles (or beer cans, wimp) What!? No empties? Well, start drinking and make some.

Finally, as I've mentioned, a little sand (or dirt if no sand is available) to fill the glass bottles partway is useful, and it is necessary if using plastic bottles or cans. Sand gives lighter containers a bit of heft, and it helps prevent glass from being shattered when struck by a Frisbee.

FIELD OF PLAY AND SETUP

Polish horseshoes is best played at the beach, which has so much helpful sand: the Wiffle ball bats are easily stuck into sand; sand goes inside the bottles; and sand provides a softer landing for a falling bottle. However, this can be played any place where 2 polelike objects can be made to stand on their own some 20 to 40 feet apart. Adjust the distance depending on the degree of difficulty you're going for.

Polish horseshoes is invariably played by 2 teams of 2 people each. It just doesn't work with any other configuration. Sorry.

Unlike horseshoes and cornhole, players on the same team stand together on the same side. Then, it's required that all players must have a drink in their hand at all times. Again, I apologize. Them's the rules.

Next, like almost every other game so far, you decide which team throws first by using a decider game. I tend to favor the coin toss, but you could also use rock-paper-scissors; bear-ninja-hunter; eeny, meeny, miny, moe; or just make up something quirky.

Then one player on the starting team throws the Frisbee toward the bottle balanced atop the opposite bat. When enacting a throw, a player should stay behind an imaginary perpendicular line extending out from the bat.

Meanwhile, the opposing team attempts to catch the Frisbee, whether it hits the bottle or not, and if the Frisbee does knock off the bottle, the opposing players *also* attempt to catch the bottle before it hits the ground.

Yes, you heard correctly: there is defense in Polish horseshoes. No, you can't block the thrower's shot. That would be too easy. But the opposing team stands behind their bat and bottle, and once the Frisbee either passes or hits the bat, they can attempt to catch the Frisbee or the Frisbee and the falling bottle.

Remember, no one on defense can touch the Frisbee until it has flown either into or past the bat and bottle.

Once a throw is made, points are tallied based on the various possible outcomes (see "Scoring" below), beers are swigged, then the other team throws the Frisbee at the first team's bottle, trying to score points, duh.

Note that as play between teams alternates, the teammates on each team must also alternate who throws the Frisbee. Failure to properly rotate throwing duties is called "shooting out of turn," and it negates any possible points scored on that turn.

Most games are played to 21, and games must be won by at least 2 points.

SCORING

Like regular horseshoes and cornhole, Polish horseshoes uses cancellation scoring. On any turn, only the throwing team can score points, but the opposing team can negate or lessen the points earned through their actions.

For the throwing team, the maximum number of points that can be scored in a throw is 3. This is done by hitting the beer bottle directly and knocking it from the opponent's pole. This play is enthusiastically known as a "dinger." If the Frisbee strikes only the pole and knocks the bottle off, this earns 2 points. Hitting the pole without knocking off the bottle (a rare occurrence) earns the throwing team 1 point.

Finally, a Frisbee that misses the pole altogether still earns 1 point, *unless the defending team catches the Frisbee.* However, note that for the throwing team to earn a point on a missed catch, the Frisbee must be at least a foot off the ground and be reasonably catchable (this rule is only applicable to Frisbees that miss the bat and bottle).

Or, to put it another way, if the defending team just stands around doing nothing, the throwing team earns at least 1 point every time. Thus, the defending team must try to catch the Frisbee on every throw. By catching the Frisbee in any scenario—either when it misses the bat or bottle or when it makes contact with them—the defending team negates 1 point.

Here's where it gets interesting: the defending team also negates 1 point if they catch the bottle before it hits the ground. Thus, on a throw that knocks off the bottle, the defending team can negate 1 point for catching either the Frisbee or the bottle, and they can negate 2 points for catching both. The ultimate feat in defensive prowess occurs when, upon a direct hit (a "dinger"), the defensive team catches both the bottle and the Frisbee. In this scenario, the throwing team hopes to earn 3 points but is forced to settle for only 1 point. Tough luck.

WARNING

If you're a badass, and if you usually drink beers that don't come in shiny aluminum bottles (I hope no Bud Platinum drinkers buy this book), then you're probably going to use glass beer bottles for Polish horseshoes. This is the traditional method—the baller method. But, as you've probably experienced at some point in your life, glass can be dangerous. For example, glass bottles and tile floors: not a good combination. Glass is hard, it's sharp, and also glass breaks, and broken glass is sharp. But even when glass doesn't break, it's hard, and an intact, flying glass bottle can hurt—to put it simply.

Plus, if you're playing with people that are good at Frisbee, dingers may be quite common. I've seen direct hits result in bottles to the face. And while there were plenty of laughs once all the blood was cleaned up, it can be, at least briefly, a scary ordeal. So, if you use glass bottles, do so at your own risk. Glass bottles may fracture, chip, or break, and this can lead to injury, an unhappy situation that my publisher's lawyers wanted me to alert you to, so you can't say I didn't warn you.

Filling a glass bottle about halfway with sand helps absorb the impact of a hit and minimize the chance of breakage. But if you really want to play it safe and prevent any possibility of breakage, (if you want to be a little wuss about it), use plastic bottles or aluminum cans (which will definitely need to be filled with sand to be heavy enough to play with).

RECOMMENDED COCKTAIL

Beer is really the only practical drink for this beach game.

BEER

INGREDIENTS

Beer

CHAPTER 9

KANJAM: THE REBELLIOUS NEPHEW

Don't fake the funk on a nasty dunk.

—SHAQUILLE O'NEAL

KanJam, oh sweet KanJam—my insatiable mistress. Horseshoes were my first love (or maybe it was croquet, or bocce). But, like a steamier version of these games, with modern charms and radical flair, KanJam stole away my heart. It can and will steal yours away too, if you want. KanJam is kind of a slut like that. But seriously.

KanJam is the American Dream embodied in lawn-sport form—it is the result of two cans, one Frisbee, and the inspiration of an everyman gym teacher. As a sport, it requires both a deft touch and Shaq-like power, while also, like Polish horseshoes, encouraging players to dive for a Frisbee while clutching a beer can—and the stench of beer splashed across one's tank top is a sign of dedication to the game.

KanJam is the brain child of a gym teacher, Paul Swisher, and his friends in upstate New York. The product of years and years of goofing around with a Frisbee and a pair of metal trashcans in backyards and parks, until one day, they thought (or one of them thought): Hey, we could make money off this—and make people supremely happy. And they were right.

Remember when I told you lawn sports were romantic? I wasn't lying.

But before KanJam was a common pastime at backyard barbecues and on collegiate quads, it was a germ of an idea swimming around in Paul Swisher's head. With the help of his friends, Swisher perfected it, patented it, and began to sell it.

Still, at first, Swisher wasn't sure where to find the customers. The answer was right under his nose. What better market for this new product than the impressionable guys and gals that Swisher already got to boss around as a gym teacher? So the company began selling KanJam sets to students in Buffalo, Rochester, and other upstate New York school systems.

The rest, as they say, is history. Soon, college students developed an emphatic obsession with the sport and began proselytizing, spreading the news via word of mouth. Today, KanJam has become an international hit, or at least a national one (I don't travel much). It's propagating faster than mosquitoes in an abandoned Florida swimming pool. It is infecting college campuses around the country like dengue fever and becoming a national hit. The kids are hot for KanJam. It doesn't forgive their love of Skrillex, but still, good for them. They got something right.

EQUIPMENT, GAME PLAY, RULES, AND STUFF
NECESSARY EQUIPMENT AND IMPORTANT ACCOUTREMENTS

All you need to play are 2 barrel-shaped containers and 1 Frisbee. There's no reason why you can't use your own Frisbee and your own set of trash cans (any size and ideally plastic, so you can cut a slit in the front), except that the ingenious creators of this game deserve your financial support. Plus, the 2 plastic barrels that come with the official game are expressly designed for KanJam and are ideal for game play, and the set comes with its own official yellow KanJam Frisbee.

FIELD OF PLAY AND SETUP

Set the 2 plastic barrels roughly 50 feet apart with the slots perfectly facing each other.

GAME PLAY

Like Polish horseshoes, KanJam can only be played by 2 teams with 2 players each. Then, teams position themselves like in regular horseshoes, with teammates stationed at opposite ends. Remember, all players must be holding a drink in one hand while playing; this ensures that players are always forced to use one hand, and one hand only, to play the game.

Flip the Frisbee to decide who goes first. Call it in the air.

Each team plays as follows: one teammate throws the Frisbee toward to their partner, who "jams" the Frisbee into the can by hitting it. The primary objective is to get the Frisbee inside the can, but hitting the outside of the can (either directly on the throw or by deflection) also scores points. As for the thrower, the aim is to float the Frisbee just over the opposite can, making for an easy dunk by the receiving teammate.

After the first throw, the same team throws again, reversing direction and roles, so both players on the same team have a chance to throw and receive in one turn. Once the first team has 2 passes, the other team takes 2 passes, and so on. Game play alternates in this way till one team scores 21 points to win.

SCORING

A "jam" or a "bucket," which is a throw and slam into the kan (Frisbee must stay in the kan until it comes to a complete stop), is equal to 3 points. A 3-point bucket does not count if the Frisbee bounces back out of the kan before it comes to a complete stop. A jam or assist that does not end up in the bottom of the kan but strikes some part of the kan and then comes to rest on the ground earns 1 point; this is often

called a "dinger." However, a direct, unassisted hit of the can by the thrower is called a "deuce" and, true to its name, earns 2 points.

If the deflector at any time grabs or catches the disc, the play is dead and no points are awarded. In KanJam, like in the NBA (theoretically, at least), there is no carrying. The slit or slot on the front of the plastic kan is called the "instant win" slot. If a player "slots it" mid-game, it's an automatic win. Game over.

Otherwise, games are played to 21 points, and a team must get 21 points exactly to win. So, for instance, if a team has 19, they must either score two "dingers" or one "deuce" to win. If a play earns points that result in a team going over 21, those points are instead subtracted from the score. Thus, if a team has 20, and then scores a 2-point deuce, the team's score goes down to 18.

As in baseball, each team gets the same number of innings, or the chance to throw an equal number of times. So if the team that started the game by throwing first is the first to score 21, the other team gets one last round of throws to match their score, thus creating a tie

game and forcing overtime. If the first team gets to 21, but it is not mathematically possible for the opponents to tie the game through the normal means of point acquisition, then that team has only one option: slot the Frisbee in the "instant win" slot, which will also create a tie and force overtime.

Overtime is a new round of play in which the first team to score 11 points wins. The team that reached 21 points first during regular play goes first in the overtime round, and the same rules apply. If teams tie again at the end of the overtime round, sudden death is forced. In sudden death, one team must beat the other team's score on each round to win; if teams tie in a sudden death round, a new sudden death round is played until one team prevails. So, for example, if the first team scores 1 "bucket" (3 points) with their 2 throws, the second team must beat 3 points to win or at least match that score to tie and play another sudden death round.

Now you're ready. Go play.

RECOMMENDED COCKTAILS

KanJam calls for canned beers. One of the great delights of the game is crumpling a freshly emptied beer can and slamming it into the kan, which also serves as a receptacle. As you collect more and more empties, the sonic evidence of a "bucket" or a "slam" or "jam" becomes more and more glorious.

BEER

INGREDIENTS

Canned beer

CHAPTER 10

STUMP: THE BACK-TO-THE-LAND OLDER BROTHER

I suppose it is tempting, if the only tool you have is a hammer, to treat everything as if it were a nail.

—ABRAHAM MASLOW

Stump straddles the line between drinking game and lawn sport. Is it a lawn game drastically improved by drinking? What lawn game isn't? Is it simply a drinking game best suited for the outdoors? Everything's better in the sun.

In its make-up—driving nails into a hunk of wood in between large swigs of beer—Stump is the most distinct of the games included in this book. There are no balls. There is no lawn or field of play. No one scores points. There are no teams or limits on the number of players. Stump accommodates whoever wants to party.

In Stump, what you get is throwing, hitting, and drinking in its purest form: toss a hammer in the air, catch it, drive a nail into a hunk of wood—ideally the round face of a tree stump—then take a large swig of beer.

Basically, you get hammered while hammering, and it is the game's very lack of elaborateness and sophistication that makes Stump so endearing. The materials needed to play are readily available at your local hardware store. An abandoned tree stump? This is slightly trickier. If you can't find any available tree stumps

or discarded cut logs suitable for the game in nearby woods or the backyards of players' houses, you can sometimes finagle scrap chunks from tree services and lumberyards for next to nothing. Then again, the DIY, outdoorsmany challenge of finding a good stump is also part of the game's charm.

No other lawn game incorporates such seemingly disparate objects into such magnificent cacophony and fun. Whack. Whack. Ding.

For me, Stump is a welcome addition to the lawn-game family because of its emphasis on hand-eye coordination, friendly competition, camaraderie, and fun. Drinking is a natural accompaniment, but not the end. You play quarters to get drunk. You play Stump to play Stump.

Stump has bona fide history, too—its roots stretching far across the Atlantic to early-nineteenth-century Germany. Stump's Germanic antecedent, the game of Hammerschlagen, was first documented at Munich's Oktoberfest in 1810. Though nearly the same as Stump—as it incorporates a stump, a hammer, lots of nails, and plenty of beer—Hammerschlagen is unique in that it usually involves a healthy number of young German lads adorned in lederhosen and sporting Robin Hood-like hats, and it requires players to hit nails using the sharp tail-end of the hammer.

Somehow, this peculiar exercise in combining drunkenness and tool-wielding mini-games became popular in America. I wonder why? Wait, I know. Drunk college kids.

Yes, Stump was thought to have first developed in its modern form at Paul Smith's College in New York, and then spread among New England's many rural liberal arts colleges, where getting hammered and throwing heavy metal objects in the air was a natural affinity. Legend has it that a slightly more sober version of the game became all the rage at a New Hampshire summer camp, and made converts out of campers and counselors alike. Then, like the colors of fall foliage, Stump slowly moved south and west by word of mouth. Today, Stump is a standard tim waster for collegians with any semblance of a social life.

EQUIPMENT, GAME PLAY, RULES, AND STUFF
NECESSARY EQUIPMENT AND IMPORTANT ACCOUTREMENTS

First, you need a stump. Truthfully, you don't need an actual stump, as it is defined in a dictionary. But you do need a healthy cut of a decent-sized tree. Midsections of a trunk are good because they are usually thick and even.

As I say, finding a good stump or round of a tree is the hardest part of this game. Explore, ask around, look for downed trees being cut into pieces to be hauled away. But don't go cut down a tree. Let's be green, just this once.

Then, you need 1 decent hammer—one with some heft and a good grip—as well as enough nails for all the players, the longer the better.

FIELD OF PLAY AND SETUP

Place the stump on the ground, cut side up.

GAME PLAY

First things first, the aim of the game is to beat everyone else's nail into the face of the stump before your nail is knocked in completely. Last nail standing wins.

Everyone who is playing should stand in front of the stump and take turns nailing their nail into the stump's surface. Nails should be hammered in enough to make them sturdy. They should be spread evenly in a circle around the surface of the stump.

To begin the game, each player "claims" a nail by placing a foot on the stump next to a nail. This will be his or her nail for the remainder of the game.

Each player must have a drink of some kind in hand at all times. This is a one-handed game, like Polish horseshoes and KanJam. The only exception to this rule is during "home improvement"; this is when, instead of taking a regular turn and attacking another player's nail, a player chooses to improve the stature of his or her nail by knocking it into a more upright posture. The player may not pull his or her nail up and farther out of the wood, but only straighten it with a few small taps.

Spin a nail to determine who goes first.

Now, players take turns trying to knock in their opponents' nails. But not with just any old hammer swing. You must use a Stump-specific "hammer toss." In a fluid, graceful motion, players must flip the hammer in the air (360-degree rotation, clockwise or counterclockwise, back flip, front flip, whatever), catch it again, and smoothly continue the motion of the flip into a strike aimed at an opponent's nail. A player gets only one chance, and if they mess it up, the hammer still moves on to the next striker.

Most importantly, the transition from the flip to the down strike must happen immediately and without hesitation. Any attempt at "cocking," "aiming," or "regripping" the hammer is not allowed and will be subject to a barrage of foul-mouthed criticism.

A player is eliminated from the game once any part of the head of his or her nail passes below the level of the surface of the stump—including when the nail is bent over the edge of the stump without

actually entering it. This is why a player might choose to spend their turn doing "home improvement" rather than bashing in someone else's nail.

Once a player is eliminated, but before he or she slinks off to go cry in the corner, the player gets a parting shot—one last hammer flip and slam on whichever nail they want. Gentlemen's rules stipulate that a retaliation shot should be taken on whoever got the retaliator out, but such a rule is not enforceable. After a person takes this parting shot, the hammer returns back to the proper rotation.

Toward the end of the game, when nails are all perilously close to death, it's not uncommon for the game to end on a series of retaliations. In this case, the last person to successfully retaliate by slamming in the last remaining nail wins.

The winner of Stump is usually awarded the privilege of pulling the nails from the stump and clearing it for a new game, while also trying to salvage any unbent nails for reuse.

SCORING

There is no scoring. Part of the genius of Stump is that it eliminates the need to count.

WARNING

If you've never dropped a hammer on your foot and want to know what it feels like, then play Stump without first practicing its idiosyncratic hammer flip and strike. If you have dropped a hammer on your foot before, then I don't need to tell you that you should practice first till you've mastered this basic move before taking your game live. Also, wearing closed-toe shoes is a good idea. Remember, one's hand-eye coordination does not improve with excessive imbibing, and all sorts of unpleasant injuries and bruises can result. Also, make sure your opponents are competent enough to be throwing hammers around. And if you don't trust someone's ability, I recommend backing away from the stump, so to allow yourself more time to react to a flying hammer.

But, just as important, don't let this warning scare you away from Stump. Like Polish horseshoes, part of the fun is doing something so patently ill-advised and surviving basically intact, through a combination of skill, foresight, and dumb luck.

RECOMMENDED COCKTAIL

Stump calls for a stiff whiskey or beer. But preferably whiskey.

Add whiskey to a glass of ice. If necessary, add a tiny splash of water. Drink. Repeat, until sufficiently buzzed.

WHISKEY

INGREDIENTS

Whiskey

THE FINAL COUNTDOWN

You've almost finished reading a book. Congrats. I mean it wasn't a novel or anything, but go ahead, give yourself a pat on the back.

At this point, you've consumed page after page filled with prose drenched in personal bias. You've read half-truths piled on top of half-truths, interspersed by strong opinions and even stronger insults. It's expected that you might be a little bit bewildered and overwhelmed by it all.

As you may have gathered, I love lawn sports. But not all lawn sports were or are created equal.

And in the wake of this book's hurricane of superlatives and name-calling—in the calm after the storm, so to speak—you might be wondering: which lawn sport is the best?

You are also probably saying to yourself: "I must play a lawn sport now!"

I feel your pain, I want to play too, but I have to keep writing (I'm on deadline).

So what sport to play? There are so many options.

Well, I'm here to offer some closure.

The competition that makes individual lawn sports so invigorating is also what makes being a lawn-sport enthusiast so enjoyable. In this conclusion, I take the pleasure of one-upmanship from the horseshoe pits and bring it to the field of critical lawn-sporting analysis itself. I have put aside a game's popularity, and challenged my own biases, in order to decide once and for all: which lawn games rule? Top to bottom, best to worst, which are the underappreciated gems, and which are sadly overrated?

Thus, after much consideration and comparative game playing, I offer the following entirely subjective ranking of this book's ten lawn games in order of awesomeness—from most awesome to somewhat less awesome.

Again, this is a subjective list, not a scientific one. But it's not put together on a whim, either. I measured each lawn sport in this list against a bevy of very real, serious criteria, such as: good-douchiness to bad-douchiness ratio, expensiveness, ease of assembly, simplicity of rules, portability of equipment, awesomeness, cool-factor, fun-factor, sophistication, inclusiveness.

I asked questions like: Which game most embodies the purest principles of lawn-sporting? Which can most quickly incorporate newcomers at a backyard barbecue? Which one most encourages its participants to dress like an asshole?

In the end, the decision-making was excruciatingly painful—pitting historical favorites against sentimental favorites against personal favorites. The old guard measured against the newcomers.

You get the point. So here goes …

1. KANJAM

As much as it pains the history major inside me, KanJam tops the list. Involving the perfect amalgamation of casualness, competitiveness, athleticism, and trash talk, KanJam was my first lawn sport obsession. It was obsession that inspired proselytizing. KanJam can be found on college campuses around the country primarily because of the passionate word-of-mouth love that it inspires in people. Croquet may have been the game that first opened my eyes to the transcendental glory of lawn games, but KanJam grew into the deep-seated love that set me on the path to becoming a lawn-sport enthusiast.

PROS: Only three pieces of equipment. The equipment is cheap, durable, and serves as a receptacle for beer cans. Yelling is encouraged.

CONS: None.

2. BOCCE

Bocce is the most classic of all lawn games. It's incredibly versatile and easy to learn. It's played in bars, on the beach, and in backyards. It ranks near the top because it can be played with utmost seriousness—clay court, intricate rules, league games, trash talking—or it can be casually enjoyed by the less experienced during a lazy day in the sun.

PROS: portable, simple, fun, awesome, great for mutual coed enjoyment

CONS: ubiquitous, may seem like you're late to the bandwagon

3. STUMP

Stump's allure is its German and New England beer-drinking, flannel-wearing heritage. You feel like a man, even if you're a woman, when you play stump, swigging beer and slamming nails into wood. It's low-key but a little dangerous. The close proximity of players encourages both camaraderie and smack talking. And while it may not seem to demand much athleticism, like most lawn games, it's an excellent test of hand-eye coordination.

PROS: makes you feel like a lumberjack, equipment easy and cheap to procure, ideal for tailgates

CONS: sometimes you take a hammer to the shinbone

4. HORSESHOES

Horseshoes was long my sentimental favorite among all lawn sports. It has somewhat fallen out of favor among the masses, and unknowing friends may turn up their nose at offers to play a game not being currently featured in the "Trends" section of their local weekly. But even if it's not currently the hip choice, horseshoes is a game that crosses racial, cultural, and socio-economic boundaries, making it forever endearing. You're just as likely to find a game of horseshoes in Nantucket as you are to find one at a Baptist church picnic is Alabama.

PROS: everyman qualities, durable equipment, ringers

CONS: sometimes you take a horseshoe to the shinbone

5. POLISH HORSESHOES

I discovered Polish horseshoes well after my first affair with plain old horseshoes, and I was enthralled. They're nothing alike. But being a lover of beer, a deft tosser of the Frisbee, and an avid appreciator of improvising games with Wiffle ball bats, I was smitten. Polish horseshoes might have ranked higher on the list except that it's really only suitable for the beach, thus it's somewhat limited.

PROS: Frisbees, beer bottles to the face, stitches, diving is encouraged, Wiffle ball bats rule

CONS: beer bottles to the face, stitches

6. CROQUET

Okay, croquet is a bitch to set up. There are all these wickets you have to stick in the ground and arrange in the proper pattern. There are all these different colored balls to keep track of. And rarely does anyone remember what the actual rules are, so you have to keep explaining them, which can make the game seem to take forever. But, if you can make it happen, and get your friends to buy in, it's one of the most elegant and interesting lawn games.

PROS: highfalutin (in a good way), sophisticated (same thing), classy (you get the point), intellectually stimulating (involves more strategy than other lawn sports)

CONS: highfalutin (in a bad way), setup is time consuming

7. PÉTANQUE

I've already professed my allegiance to bocce. If you want to play a ball-rolling game, that's the one that's easiest and most versatile. Pétanque is the best second choice, since it's the most similar. Its rules are almost identical. Where it falls short is the need for a specific playing surface and the fussy delivery. That said, the adoration the game receives from cigar-chomping European expats in city parks makes it particularly appealing—in the right circumstances.

PROS: you can pretend it's bocce

CONS: why don't you just play bocce?

8. CORNHOLE

If you read this, and didn't skip to the end to find out what happened (cheater), then you might be a little tired of the verbal whooping cornhole has received so far. It's really not that offensive of a game. But it's everywhere, and for no good reason. I have a personal aversion to people, places, and things whose popularity far outweighs their true quality. Sorry cornhole, you seem popular, but you're overrated. There are worse ways to spend an afternoon, and cornhole certainly provides a ready arena for friendly competition, but if you're looking for an interesting game in itself, this isn't it.

PROS: readily available at tailgates and parties, easy to learn, easy to play

CONS: boring

9. LAWN BOWLING

Lawn bowling might be cooler if it hadn't been exclusively claimed by retirement communities in South Florida. Elsewhere (Europe), lawn bowling enjoys the participation of a whole range of age groups. But as stated before, lawn bowling seems like an unnecessary and even more elaborate way to play bocce. It requires huge fields of perfectly mown grass, and the fields are often accompanied by warning signs telling players to keep their voices down and demanding that you wear all white. This kind of snobbery should only be tolerated at croquet tournaments.

PROS: it's kind of like bocce, has lots of history

CONS: it's not practical, like, it's really not practical

10. BADMINTON

Badminton's slight bit of history having enamored upperclass Brits at the turn of the 19th century earned it a place in this book. But let's be honest, badminton wasn't even fun in middle school gym class. So it's hard to understand how it could be fun now, with so many other options. I mean seriously, if you want to play a net sport, just go play tennis or volleyball or ping-pong—all great sports. Just anything but badminton.

PROS: you get to say "shuttlecock" as much as you want

CONS: you feel like an asshole the whole time you play; also you have to transport, set up, and then take down a giant net

UNAPOLOGETIC OMISSIONS

Much like the X Games—which continues to invent asinine new sports each year, like ice biking and snowmobile hockey, in an effort to seem cool and build TV viewership—the lawn game family seems to grow larger and larger each year for no good reason, with patents being filed for some ludicrous new amalgamation of plastic. It's not that there's no room for ingenuity and invention in lawn-sporting. There's just no room for shitty inventions. Quality over quantity, guys, quality over quantity.

Below is a list of a few of those *other* lawn games, which enjoy small pockets of enthusiasm in various parts of the world, but fail to make any meaningful contributions to the lawn-sport family.

KUBB – A Swedish game that involves, literally, throwing wooden sticks at wooden blocks. No kidding. Kubb is a case study in elaborate stupidity.

LADDER GOLF – Another example of a game trying to do too much. I mean, really? All ladder golf does is attach two balls by a string and throw them at some PVC-pipe contraption. It doesn't help that I've only ever seen double-popped-collared douche bags playing this game.

LAWN DARTS – Hypothetically, lawn darts sounds like a lot of fun. Until someone takes a dart to the skull. For legal reasons, I can do nothing but discourage participation in this now-outlawed game.

WASHER PITCHING – Almost identical to cornhole, but more annoying. Instead of throwing beanbags into a hole, you throw small metal washers into a hole.

FLIMSEE – A bastardized form of Polish horseshoes. Flimsee takes the throwing a Frisbee at a pole and object idea and tweaks it ever so slightly in a sleazy attempt to make money, not add value to the world of lawn sports.

QUOITS – An antiquated version of horseshoes. Like washer pitching, but instead of throwing washers into a hole, you throw them onto a stake. In the grand survival-of-the-fittest evolution of lawn games, horseshoes won out, so get over it.

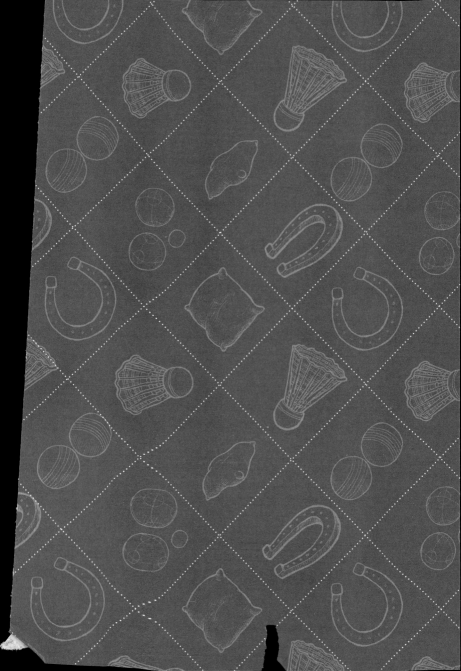

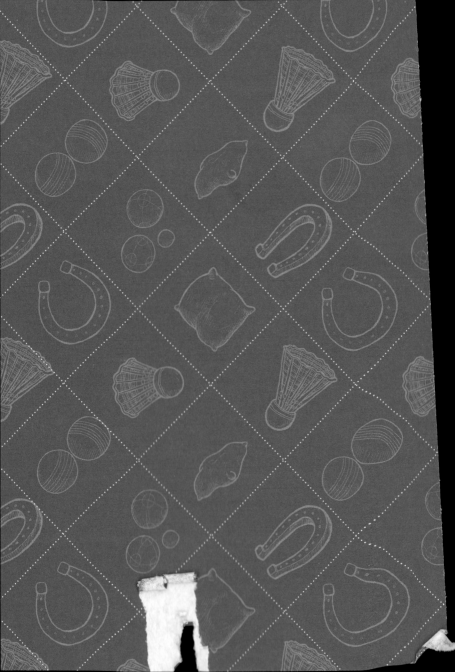